The Book of Revelation
Discipleship Lessons

and Bible Study Commentary for Personal Devotional Use, Small Groups or Sunday School Classes, and Sermon Preparation for Pastors and Teachers

JesusWalk® Bible Study Series
by Dr. Ralph F. Wilson
Director, Joyful Heart Renewal Ministries

Additional books, and reprint licenses are available at:
www.jesuswalk.com/books/revelation.htm

Free Participant Guide handout sheets are available at:
www.jesuswalk.com/revelation/revelation-lesson-handouts.pdf

JesusWalk® Publications
Loomis, California

Copyright © 2004, 2011, Ralph F. Wilson. All rights reserved. May not be copied or reproduced without explicit permission.

Paperback
ISBN-13: 978-0-9832310-5-9
ISBN-10: 0983231052

Library of Congress Control Number: 2011911872

Library of Congress subject heading:
    Bible. – N.T. – Revelation.

Suggested Classifications
    Dewey Decimal System: 228
    Library of Congress: BS2825

Published by JesusWalk® Publications, P.O. Box 565, Loomis, CA 95650-0565, USA.

JesusWalk is a registered trademark and Joyful Heart is a trademark of Joyful Heart Renewal Ministries.

Bible verses are quoted from the New International Version (International Bible Society, 1973, 1978), used by permission. Also from The Revised Standard Version (Division of Christian Education of the National Council of Churches of Christ in the USA, 1946). The 2011 edition was only slightly revised from the 2004 edition.

110805

Preface

Many people study Revelation for the wrong reasons. They want to figure out when Jesus will return. They are fascinated and horrified with the graphic symbols, at the same time repelled and attracted. Let me clarify our approach in this study.

Our goal is to learn the powerful message of the Book to Christians today, and learn what its message was to churches at the end of the First Century.

Revelation cannot be taken literally. It is symbolic, not literal teaching. This doesn't mean it isn't true, only that it must be understood differently than the narrative of the Gospels and Acts, or the letters of Paul and other Apostles. It is full of symbols and thus can only be understood if the meaning of the symbols is probed and understood.

William Blake, "Four and Twenty Elders Casting Their Crowns before the Divine Throne" (1803-05), pen and watercolor, Tate Gallery, London.

The timing of the Tribulation and Rapture is only a minor theme. If these areas are your main interests, please don't enroll for this study. (Incidentally, I am pre-millennial, mid-trib, though I see a good case for amillennialism. I think that the "secret rapture" taught in the *Left Behind* series rests on a pretty shaky interpretation of scripture.) We'll explore the various views, but frankly, they aren't very central to understanding Revelation. We will consider but *not* be debating different views of the rapture.

My interest is **to help serious disciples understand and heed the message of Revelation**, not to tickle your intellectual curiosity. I want you to come away a changed person – sobered some, since Revelation is a pretty sober Book – but more than that, filled with a zeal to be a faithful witness to Christ in your generation.

Having said that, I hope you will put away your preconceived doctrines, open your mind, and plumb with me the depths of Revelation. I don't understand everything in this Book – no one really does. But I'll help you understand its basic message.

Revelation is a powerful revelation to the churches designed to help shake us out of our spiritual lethargy and stimulate us to be faithful witnesses not matter what persecution we face. May you be gripped by the message of Revelation as I have been – now and for the rest of your life.

God bless you,
Dr. Ralph F. Wilson

Table of Contents

Preface	3
Table of Contents	5
Reprint Guidelines	8
References and Abbreviations	9
Introduction to the Book of Revelation	**11**
Influence	11
Type of Literature	12
Date and Author	12
Intended Readers	13
Purpose and Theme	13
Structure	13
Interpretation	14
Principles of Interpretation	15
Translation	15
How This Study Works	16
1. Christ in the Midst of the Lampstands (chapter 1)	**18**
Prologue (1:1-3)	19
Greetings (1:4-5a)	20
Numbers in the Bible	20
Doxology and Response (1:5b-7)	21
Tribulation (1:9)	22
Geography (1:9-11)	23
Symbolic Representation of Christ (1:12-20)	23
2. Letters to the Seven Churches (chapters 2-3)	**26**
The Church in Ephesus (2:1-7)	26
The Church in Smyrna (2:8-11)	28
The Church in Pergamum (2:12-17)	29
The Church in Thyatira (2:18-29)	29
The Church in Sardis (3:1-6)	30
The Church in Philadelphia (3:7-13)	31
The Church in Laodicea (3:14-22)	32

3. The Lion That Is the Lamb (chapters 4-5) — 34

4. The 144,000 (chapters 6-10) — 39
  The Seven Seals (6:1-17) — 40
  The 144,000 (7:1-8) — 42
  The Great Multitude in White Robes (7:9-17) — 44
  The Seventh Seal and the Golden Censer (8:1-5) — 46
  The Seven Trumpets (8:6-9:21) — 46
  The Angel and the Little Scroll (10:1-11) — 48

5. By the Blood of the Lamb (chapters 11-13) — 51
  The Two Witnesses (11:1-14) — 51
  The Seventh Trumpet (11:15-19) — 55
  The Woman and the Dragon (12:1-13:1a) — 55
  The Beast out of the Sea (13:1b-10) — 58
  The Beast out of the Earth (13:11-18) — 59

6. Alas, Babylon! (chapters 14-18) — 62
  The Lamb and the 144,000 (14:1-5) — 62
  The Three Angels (14:6-13) — 63
  The Harvest of the Earth (14:14-20) — 64
  Seven Angels with Seven Plagues (15:1-8) — 65
  The Seven Bowls of God's Wrath (16:1-21) — 66
  The Woman on the Beast (17:1-18) — 68
  The Fall of Babylon (18:1-24) — 69

7. The Millennium (chapters 19-20) — 71
  Praise from the Heavenly Multitude (19:1-10) — 71
  The Rider on the White Horse (19:11-21) — 73
  The Thousand Years (20:1-15) — 74

8. We Shall See His Face (chapters 21-22) — 80
  The New Jerusalem (21:1-27) — 80
  The River of Life (22:1-6) — 84
  Jesus Is Coming (22:7-21) — 85

Appendix 1: Questions for Group Participants — 87
  1. Christ in the Midst of the Lampstands (chapter 1) — 88
  2. Letters to the Seven Churches (chapters 2-3) — 91
  3. The Lion That Is the Lamb (chapters 4-5) — 92
  4. The 144,000 (chapters 6-10) — 93

5. By The Blood of the Lamb (chapters 11-13)	94
6. Alas, Babylon! (chapters 14-18)	96
7. The Millennium (chapters 19-20)	97
8. We Shall See His Face (chapters 21-22)	98

Appendix 2: Charts — 99

Appendix 3. Songs and Hymns Based on Revelation — 109

Reprint Guidelines

Copying the Handouts. In some cases, small groups or Sunday school classes would like to use these notes to study this material. That's great. An appendix provides copies of handouts designed for classes and small groups. There is no charge whatsoever to print out as many copies of the handouts for participants as you need. All charts and notes are copyrighted and must bear the line:

"Copyright © 2011, Ralph F. Wilson. All rights reserved. Reprinted by permission."

You may not resell these notes to other groups or individuals outside your congregation. You may, however, charge people in your group enough to cover your copying costs. Free Participant Guide handout sheets are available at:

www.jesuswalk.com/revelation/revelation-lesson-handouts.pdf

Copying the book (or the majority of it) in your congregation or group, you are requested to purchase a reprint license for each book. A Reprint License, $2.50 for each copy is available for purchase at

www.jesuswalk.com/books/revelation.htm

Or you may send a check to:

Dr. Ralph F. Wilson
JesusWalk Publications
PO Box 565
Loomis, CA 95650, USA

The Scripture says,

"The laborer is worthy of his hire" (Luke 10:7) and "Anyone who receives instruction in the word must share all good things with his instructor" (Galatians 6:6).

However, if you are from a third world country or an area where it is difficult to transmit money, please make a small contribution instead to help the poor in your community.

References and Abbreviations

Alford	Henry Alford, *The Greek Testament* (Seventh edition, 1849-1860. reprinted Moody Press, 4 volumes, 1958, 1968)
BDAG	Walter Bauer and Frederick W. Danker, *A Greek-English Lexicon of the New Testament and Other Early Christian Literature* (Third Edition, 2000; based on a previous English editions by W.F. Arndt, F.W. Gingrich, and F.W. Danker; University of Chicago Press, 1957, 1979)
BDB	Francis Brown, S.R. Driver, and Charles A. Briggs (eds.), *A Hebrew and English Lexicon of the Old Testament* (Oxford: Clarendon Press, 1907). Used in an electronic edition.
Beale	Gregory K. Beale, *The Book of Revelation* (New International Greek Testament Commentary; Eerdmans, 1999)
Beasley-Murray	G. R. Beasley-Murray, *Revelation* (The New Century Bible Commentary; Eerdmans, 1974, 1978)
Bruce	Bruce, F. F., "Revelation" in *A New Testament Commentary*, ed. G. C. D. Howley (Eerdmans, 1969)
Caird	G.B. Caird, *The Revelation of St. John the Divine* (Harper's New Testament Commentaries; Harper & Row, 1966; reprinted by Hendrickson, 1993)
DLNT	*Dictionary of the Later New Testament and Its Developments*, edited by Ralph P. Martin and Peter H. Davids (InterVarsity Press, 1997)
Hendriksen	William Hendriksen, *More Than Conquerors* (Baker, 1939)
Hughes	Philip Edgcumbe Hughes, *The Book of the Revelation: A Commentary* (Eerdmans, 1990)
ISBE	Geoffrey W. Bromiley (general editor), *The International Standard Bible Encyclopedia* (Eerdmans, 1979-1988; fully revised from the 1915 edition)

KJV	King James Version (Authorized Version, 1611)
Ladd	George E. Ladd, *A Commentary on the Revelation of John* (Eerdmans, 1972)
Merriam-Webster	*Merriam-Webster's Collegiate Dictionary* (Tenth Edition; Merriam-Webster, 1993)
Morris	Leon Morris, *The Revelation of St. John* (Tyndale NT Commentaries; Eerdmans, 1969, revised 1987)
Mounce	Robert H. Mounce, *The Book of Revelation* (New International Commentary on the NT; Eerdmans, 1977). ISBN 0802825370, hardback 475 pages.
NASB	New American Standard Bible (The Lockman Foundation, 1960-1988)
NIV	New International Version (International Bible Society, 1973, 1978)
NJB	New Jerusalem Bible (Darton, Longman & Todd Ltd, 1985)
NRSV	New Revised Standard Version (Division of Christian Education of the National Council of Churches of Christ, USA, 1989)
RSV	Revised Standard Version (Division of Christian Education of the National Council of Churches of Christ in the USA, 1946).
TDNT	Gerhard Kittel and Gerhard Friedrich (editors), Geoffrey W. Bromiley (translator and editor), *Theological Dictionary of the New Testament* (Eerdmans, 1964-1976; translated from *Theologisches Wörterbuch zum Neuen Testament*, ten volume edition)
Thayer	Joseph Henry Thayer, *Greek-English Lexicon of the New Testament* (Associated Publishers and Authors, n.d., reprinted from 1889 edition)
Wilcock	Michael Wilcock, *I Saw Heaven Opened* (The Bible Speaks Today; InterVarsity Press, 1975, 1988)

Introduction to the Book of Revelation

Revelation was originally written to guide and encourage a persecuted Church. While Americans may not experience much persecution for their Christian faith, the opposite has been true around the world in the last century. The 20th Century saw more martyrs for the Christian faith than all the previous centuries put together. Dictators such as Idi Amin in Uganda, Stalin in the Soviet Union, and Mao Zedong in China were responsible for killing millions of believers in order to suppress Christianity. They didn't succeed. A resurgence of radical Islam and fundamentalist Hinduism imperil Christians in many lands today. The message of Revelation is very relevant indeed for our generation.

Influence

The Book of Revelation has exerted a huge influence on the Christian Church and Western thought. During cycles of the Black Plague in the Middle Ages, Europe was sure it was experiencing the plagues mentioned in Revelation 6. Many of the phrases and symbols in Revelation have found their way into English vocabulary and imagination – "pearly gates" (21:21), "lukewarm" (3:16), "overcomers" (2:7, etc.), "Alpha and Omega" (1:8; 21:6; 22:13), "the second death" (2:11), "book of life" (3:5), "666" (13:18), the Millennium (20:1-6), and the "lake of fire" (19:20; 20:10, 15), to name just a few.

William Holman Hunt (Pre-Raphaelite British painter (1827-1910), "Light of the World" (1853), Keble College, Oxford. The painting illustrates Revelation 3:20. A later copy is also displayed at St. Paul's Cathedral, London.

Type of Literature

It's not hard to see that Revelation is very different than anything else in the New Testament. Actually, it is a different genre or type of literature. The other New Testament books are Gospels (evangelistic biographies of Jesus' life and ministry), Epistles (letters designed to guide individuals and churches to better live out the Christian life), and the Book of Acts (a history of the early church).

You're familiar with different genres or types of songs – Country and Western, classical, soft rock, Big Band, Negro spiritual, etc. Each has its own distinctive approach and style. Literature types can include biography, history, historical fiction, romance fiction, poetry, etc. Each type of literature must be considered and understood within its own genre.

The Book of Revelation is an example of apocalyptic literature, a type of Jewish-Christian writing that flourished after the exile, especially between 250 BC and 150 AD. The chief example in the Old Testament is Daniel 7-13, with some proto-apocalyptic passages found in Ezekiel; Isaiah; Joel; and Zechariah. In addition to these, scholars have found 14 Jewish and 23 Christian documents of this type. This genre of literature communicates about the End Time through visions and symbolic language.

We don't have any good examples of this highly symbolic style in modern literature. John Bunyan's *Pilgrim's Progress* (1678) is a complex allegory presented as a dream. Jonathan Swift's *Gulliver's Travels* (1726) is a highly symbolic satire of his age. But these are centuries old. The best current examples of using symbols to communicate are to be found in political cartoons. Here you see donkeys and elephants interacting in various ways. Political cartoons use recognizable symbols to make a point. So does the Book of Revelation and apocalyptic literature of its era.

To understand the symbols used, however, requires a familiarity with the Old Testament. You'll see many Old Testament references in the notes. Feel free to look them up to learn more.

Date and Author

The earliest church writers are unanimous that "John" (1:1) who recorded this revelation was John the Apostle, the son of Zebedee (Justin Martyr, *Dialogue with Trypho* 81, Irenaeus, *Against Heresies* iii.11.1; iv.20.11; v.35.2; Tertullian, *Against Marcion* iii.14.3). I lean in this direction, too. There are many similarities between Revelation and the Gospel of John, but also many differences, including grammar. Since John doesn't identify himself as an apostle, it is also possible that he is another John, sometimes called

John the Elder. We just aren't sure, though I lean believe this is John the Apostle. Fortunately, however, exactly which John is the author doesn't really affect how the book should be interpreted. Whoever he was, he had been exiled to the Isle of Patmos for his preaching (1:9). Most scholars believe that Revelation was written during the persecution of the later years of the reign of Domitian (AD 81-96), around AD 95.

Intended Readers

The seven churches mentioned in chapters 2 and 3 cluster around Ephesus, the chief city of Asia Minor, the traditional pastoral residence of John the Apostle later in his life (Eusebius, *Church History* 5.8.4). The book was no doubt intended to both warn and encourage these First Century readers. However, though conditions which characterized the last decade of the First Century AD are the focus of Revelation, the book has an important message for all believers who await the return of Christ.

Purpose and Theme

The purpose of the Revelation is to jolt those Christians who are compromising with idolatry out of their spiritual anesthesia so that they will perceive the spiritual danger they are in and repent (Beale). It is also designed to comfort and encourage the faithful, witnessing church in its struggle against the forces of evil. Assurance is given that: God sees their tears (7:17; 21:4); their prayers rule the world! (8:3-4); death ushers them into a glorious heaven (14:13; 20:4); their final victory is assured (15:2); their Christ lives and reigns forever, who governs the world in the interest of His church (5:7-8); and that He is coming again to take his people to Himself (chapters. 21-22).

The theme of the book is the victory of Christ and of His church over the dragon (Satan) and his helpers. The theme is stated in 17:14:

> "They will make war on the Lamb, and the Lamb will conquer them, for He is Lord of lords and King of kings, and those with Him are called and chosen and faithful."

Structure

The book seems to be divided into seven sections which can easily be distinguished from each other.

1. Christ in the midst of the Seven Golden Lampstands (chapters 1-3)

    a. Christ the eternal One (chapter 1)

  b. Letters to the Seven Churches (chapters 2-3)

2. The Scroll with the Seven Seals (chapters 4-7)
3. The Seven Trumpets of Judgment (chapters 8-11)
4. The Seven Mystic Figures (chapters 12-14)
5. The Seven Bowls of Wrath and Judgment of Babylon (chapters 15-18)
6. The Consummation (chapters 19-20)
7. The New Heavens and the New Earth (chapters 21-22)

Two major divisions:

1. **Chapters 1-11 The struggle on earth**: The church persecuted by the world. The church is avenged, protected, and victorious.
2. **Chapters 12-22 The deeper spiritual background**: The Christ (and the church) persecuted by the dragon (Satan) and his helpers. Christ and His church are victorious.

Interpretation

Historically there have been four major divisions of interpretation (with many variations):

1. The **preterite**–everything has already been fulfilled.
2. The **historical**–the predictions are in the process of fulfillment.
3. The **futurist**–all predictions are in the future.
4. The **spiritual**–the events described are only symbols of spiritual realities and struggles, without any literal or historical application.

John was told, "Now write what you see, what is and what is to take place hereafter" (1:19). After the letters to the seven churches he is told, "Come up hither, and I will show you what must take place after this" (4:1). As I consider the text, I find it necessary sometimes to hold the preterite view (this was fulfilled in the first century or shortly thereafter); sometimes the historical view (this was fulfilled in the middle ages, or is in the process of fulfillment); sometimes the futurist view (this is still yet to come); or perhaps even the spiritual view (that these events are symbols of spiritual realities and struggles).

Introduction to the Book of Revelation

Principles of Interpretation

1. The Revelation is rooted in **contemporaneous events and circumstances**. Its symbols should be interpreted in light of the conditions which prevailed when the book was written.
2. Revelation shares a characteristic of Bible prophets, in that **contemporary historical events** are seen as a **type of, or a prelude to, the great Day of the Lord** in the latter days. Often they do this without a chronological distinction between the two.
3. **John is an artist in words and symbols**. We are to look for the meaning conveyed by each symbol in that symbol itself. It doesn't really matter whether or not the symbols can be visualized or reconciled.
4. **I hesitant to speculate** which, if any, *current* events, nations, or political figures are referred to in Revelation. The history of interpretation is littered with hundreds of mistaken identities. Rather I am looking for the basic structure of events and principles of faith and action for Christians in the End Times.
5. **I am reluctant to superimpose upon Revelation a preconceived system of interpretation** (that is, pre-, post-, a-millennial, or pre-, mid, or post-tribulation rapture). In this study we'll consider these various alternatives. The time to synthesize the *whole* teaching of the Bible about the End Times is after we have carefully analyzed each portion on its own terms.
6. I see Revelation as **not a simple chronology of events from chapters 4 through 22**; rather as a **series of visions which may parallel each other** chronologically, but which emphasize different aspects of divine truth. This view is called "parallelism".
7. I believe that **we can learn much from Revelation, even though there are parts we do not understand**. I consider myself a student of the book, not a master of it. I believe God will reveal some of the hidden parts of Revelation to Christians only when we need to know them. Until then, all our speculations are a waste of time and can get in the way of learning.

Translation

These lessons are based primarily on the Revised Standard Version (RSV) translation that I was using when I first wrote the study notes, though some portions of the notes include the New International Version (NIV). However, any modern study Bible should work well as you study Revelation, except a paraphrase, such as the *Living Bible* or *The Message*.

How This Study Works

We've tried to design this study of Revelation so you'll be able to grasp the real message of Revelation. Here's how you can get the most out of this study.

1. **Read the Book of Revelation** several times, asking God to help you understand what you are reading.
2. **Study notes, questions, and charts** are designed to help you learn. Look up the verses that interest you. The questions and charts are available separately in Appendix 1 and Appendix 2 of this book. Even if you don't print out the whole book, print out these. Take notes on the sheets provided.
3. **Answer the Questions.** Answer the questions numbered Q1, Q2, Q3, etc. A study group or Sunday school class can discuss the questions during class. If you're studying on your own, I recommend studying one question each day, one lesson each week. This daily thinking on Revelation will keep your mind focused on this book and have a great cumulative impact on your life. Try to answer these questions in your own words. Don't just parrot back the words you find in the notes. Think this through for yourself. These questions are designed to help you apply the truths of Revelation to your own life and to your church.
4. **Post Your Answers on the Joyful Heart Bible Study Forum**. A unique aspect of this study is an online Forum where you can read others' answers and post your own. The process of reflecting, writing, and reading their answers will help reinforce and establish these truths in your heart.

www.joyfulheart.com/forums/index.php?showforum=107

You can find full instructions online explaining how to register and post your answers (www.joyfulheart.com/forums/instructions.htm).

As you can imagine, people have disagreements about the Book of Revelation. That's okay, but I expect each participant in the Forum to scrupulously follow the Bible Study Forum Guidelines (www.jesuswalk.com/admin/pu_forum_guidelines.htm) Especially, let your words be flooded with love, not disputation. You are free to disagree with me and one another, but do so in love and tolerance toward one another. The Forum is not a fighting place, but an extension of Christ's Church online. Our goal is to learn and grow in Christ's likeness.

It's exciting to meet other people who are involved in this Bible study. Feel free to **check in** and share a bit about yourself, and what state and country you are from. Be discrete about sharing private things about yourself. Be aware that some people on the Forum will have written their answers months before. Others will you're your responses months after you have written them. Even so, it is a way to learn along with others. www.joyfulheart.com/forums/index.php?showtopic=117

It is my prayer that as you study Revelation you continually call upon Jesus, who gave this vision (1:1-2), to show you how its message should affect your life and thinking. Mere knowledge is useless; knowledge that we absorb into our living and value system – that knowledge is worth much.

Prayer

Father, teach us together as we study this special, awesome, and unique portion of your Word. Change us as a result. In Jesus' name, we pray. Amen.

1. Christ in the Midst of the Lampstands (chapter 1)

Revelation is the most difficult book in the New Testament to understand, so it's best to begin our study with prayer and humility.

> "Lord, help me understand what you are saying to me in the Book of Revelation. And help my life to be more faithful to you as a result. In Jesus' name, I pray. Amen."

The first chapter introduces several of the key themes of Revelation:

1. Faithful testimony and witness (1:2)
2. Grace offered to us in Jesus' death for our sins (1:5-6)
3. Judgment to those who reject Christ (1:7)
4. Christ's return (1:7)
5. The eternal nature of the Father and Son (1:4, 8, 17-18)
6. The glory of the exalted Christ (1:12-16)
7. Christ's concern for local congregations (1:20)

Albrecht Dürer, "Christ Among the Lampstands" (1498), woodcut, 11 x 18"

1. Christ in the Midst of the Lampstands (chapter 1)

There's more, of course, but that's just the first chapter. Now I invite you to study the text carefully and look up the Scripture references. Revelation, the last book in the Bible, draws together strings from all the main themes from Genesis, Exodus, Numbers, Isaiah, Daniel, Ezekiel, and many New Testament books as it weaves a striking and fantastic tapestry of the End Times. I encourage you to answer the questions that are in the boxes numbered Q1, Q2, etc. The URL after each of these questions allows you to post your answer on our online Forum and to read others' answers to the questions.

Prologue (1:1-3)

1:1 The word **"revelation"** is Greek *apocalypsis*, literally "uncovering." Here it means "making fully known, revelation, disclosure" (BDAG 112). We see here a statement of purpose for the book.

1:2 **"Testify," "testimony,"** and **"witness"** are key ideas in this book. Greek *martureō* means "to confirm or attest something on the basis of personal knowledge or belief, bear witness, be a witness" (BDAG 617-620). The related word *marturia*, "testimony," can also refer to sworn testimony in court. Our English word "martyr," "one who testifies at the cost of life" comes from this Greek word group. This word group appears many times in Revelation: 1:2, 5, 9; 2:13; 3:14; 6:9; 11:3, 7; 12:11, 17; 17:6; 19:10; 20:4; 22:16; 22:18, 20. See also 15:5.

Q1. Revelation is written to encourage and strengthen a church facing intense persecution. Why is the theme of testimony and witness so important to that purpose? How is Jesus as the "faithful witness" (1:5) supposed to encourage us? Why are we afraid to be clear witnesses in a culture where we aren't persecuted?
http://www.joyfulheart.com/forums/index.php?showtopic=107

1:3 Revelation is called a **"prophecy"** (also 22:7, 10, 18, 19. Compare 19:10). Prophecy in the OT included exhortation to godly living as well as occasional predictions of the future.

"Blessed." This is the first of seven blessings pronounced in Revelation. Others are found in 14:13; 16:15; 19:9; 20:6; 22:7, 14.

"Keep what is written therein." Indicates that the work was considered as moral instruction and not only prediction.

Greetings (1:4-5a)

Revelation is a circular letter sent to the seven churches in Asia Minor addressed in chapters 2 and 3.

"Is and was and is to come." Look up God's self-revelation in Exodus 3:14 showing His eternal nature. See also Hebrews 13:8. Then list the ways this concept is taught in Revelation 1:

verse 4

verse 8

verses 17-18

1:4-5 Write how each Person of the Trinity is described:
  1. Father

  2. Son

  3. Holy Spirit
     (see 3:1; 4:5; 5:6)

Numbers in the Bible

Numbers in the Bible and other ancient literature often have symbolic or cultic meaning, sometimes used with literal *and* symbolic meanings simultaneously. These aren't "magic" numbers, but symbolic with sacred implications to the ancient Semitic culture.

Seven is the sacred number of completeness, perfection, fullness. Jesus told Peter to forgive 70 x 7 – that is, completely, without end. The number seven is particularly predominant in Revelation: churches (1:4, 11, 20), lampstands (1:12, 13; 2:1); stars (1:16, 20; 2:1; 3:1); torches (4:5); horns, eyes (5:6); seals (5:1; 6:1); angels (8:2, 6; 15:1, 6-8; 17:1; 21:9); trumpets (8:2, 6); thunders (10:3); heads (12:3; 31:1; 17:3, 7, 9); crowns (12:3); bowls (15:7; 16:1; 17:1; 21:9); heads of state (17:9, see verse 11); plagues (15:1, 6, 8; 21:9); mountains (17:9); seven thousand (11:13).

1. Christ in the Midst of the Lampstands (chapter 1)

1:4 The **"seven spirits"** probably refer to the completeness and universality of the working of God's Holy Spirit (Beasley-Murray), as the seven churches typify and indicate the whole church (Alford).

Doxology and Response (1:5b-7)

1:5 "Faithful witness." As such, He is the model for persecuted Christians to follow (see John 3:32; 18:37).

"Firstborn" refers to "sovereignty, first place, heir," due to Christ being the first to be resurrected to glory (Romans 8:29; Colossians 1:18; Psalm 89:27).

"Ruler of the kings of the earth." This title was vindicated by his resurrection (Philippians 2:10-11). The usurper had claimed this honor (Matthew 4:8-10; John 12:31; 14:30; 16:11), but it rightfully belongs to the One who created it and will be revealed as King of kings (17:14; 19:16). He is sovereign and will ultimately prevail.

"Loosed us by his blood" is probably the earliest text rather than KJV "washed us in his blood." The difference between the two is probably a copyist's error: *lousanti* is mistakenly written for *lusanti*. In any case the image of being washed in Christ's blood is seen in 7:14. What continuing (present tense) love this suggests!

"A kingdom, priests," not "kings and priests" as in KJV, which is also likely a copyist's error. However, in a parallel passage (5:10) this kingdom of priests "shall reign on the earth" on behalf of the Messiah (see 1 Peter 2:9 and Exodus 19:6).

"Coming with the clouds." This is central to Jesus understanding of himself as the heavenly Son of Man figure of Daniel (Daniel 7:13; Matthew 24:30; Acts 1:9, 11).

"Every eye shall see him who pierced him." (Zechariah 12:10; Matthew 24:30).

1:8 "Alpha and Omega." First and last letters of the Greek alphabet (Hebrews 12:2).

Q2. What does 1:8 tell us about the Father? The Father is the speaker here in 1:8 and in 21:6. But Jesus is the speaker in 1:17 and 22:12-13. What is the significance of this for our understanding of who Jesus is?
http://www.joyfulheart.com/forums/index.php?showtopic=108

Tribulation (1:9)

1:9 "Share with you in Jesus the tribulation." "Tribulation" is Greek *thlipsis* (verses 21, 29), "trouble that inflicts distress, oppression, affliction, tribulation" (BDAG 457). "Tribulation" refers here to the suffering which accompanies faithfulness to Christian principles (John 16:33; Acts 14:22; 2 Timothy 3:12), but extends to include the final period of intensified affliction which precedes the establishment of the kingdom (Mounce). Ladd writes that tribulation here is "especially the great tribulation at the end, which will be only the intensification of what the church has suffered throughout all history" (p. 30).

Q3. In what countries are Christians presently experiencing tribulation or persecution for the faith? How can the Book of Revelation be a comfort and encouragement to them?

http://www.joyfulheart.com/forums/index.php?showtopic=109

A great object of (sometimes foolish) debate is whether the Church will go through the "great tribulation," by which some mean God's judgment upon the sinful world at the end time. We won't resolve this issue here, but let's distinguish two concepts. You'll find a lot of clarity when you distinguish between (1) God's wrath in his righteous judgment of sin and (2) Satan's wrath against Christians resulting in persecution. Record your observations on the following verses, but don't share your observations in the Forum. We won't debate chronologies of the tribulation there, since it serves little spiritual purpose.

Matthew 24:9, 21-22, 29. "Tribulation" is the Greek word *thlipsis*.

1 Thessalonians 5:9 "Wrath" is the Greek noun *orgē*, "strong indignation directed at wrongdoing, with focus on retribution, wrath, of God's future judgment" (BDAG 720-721)

Revelation 2:9, 22 NIV afflictions, suffering = tribulation, Greek *thlipsis*.

Revelation 6:9-11
   with 7:9-14. In 7:14 tribulation, Greek *thlipsis*.

2 Thessalonians 1:4-10
   NIV trials = tribulations, Greek *thlipsis*

1. Christ in the Midst of the Lampstands (chapter 1)

Geography (1:9-11)

1:10 "In the Spirit," a state of spiritual exultation and acuity in the spiritual realm (2 Corinthians 12:2-4 and Revelation 4:1-2).

"On the Lord's day," that is, the day of Jesus' resurrection, Sunday, the first day of the week, when Christians met for worship and the Lord's Supper (Acts 20:7-11, 1 Corinthians 16:2). The term "Lord's Day" was used in early Christian writings such as the *Didache* 14:1 and the *Letter of Ignatius to the Magnesians* 9:1 (Here the "Lord's Day" is distinguished from the Sabbath day. See "Paul K. Jewett, "Lord's Day," ISBE 3:158-160.)

"Patmos" is an island just off the coast of Asia Minor (present-day Turkey) when John had been exiled for his Christian faith, and where he received this revelation.

1:11 "Seven churches" are all found in the western part of Asia Minor, perhaps churches for which John had apostolic responsibility. Revelation is sent as a circular letter to these churches, which are discussed more fully in lesson 2.

Symbolic Representation of Christ (1:12-20)

It's easy to over-interpret symbols. Some of the creatures depicted in Revelation are bizarre when their characteristics are depicted graphically. John's allusions are sometimes given for their symbolic meaning, but are often "for their evocative and emotive power ... to set the echoes of memory and association ringing" (Caird). For example, the symbolic representation of Christ in this passage has several characteristics in common with the angelic character who appeared to Daniel in Daniel 10:6.

1:12 "Golden lampstands" = churches. See Matthew 5:14-16 to understand the relationship between lampstands and faithful witness.

1:13a "Son of man." This was Jesus' self-designation during his ministry. "Son of man" probably is a Hebrew way of saying "human being." But when "Son of man" is identified with the figure from Daniel 7:13, who comes on the clouds, it is an exalted title indeed.

1:13b "Feet like bronze," – glowing!

1:14 "White as white wool," used to describe the Ancient of Days in Daniel 7:9. Purity and glory.

"Eyes like a flame of fire." Penetrating insight (2:18; 19:12; Daniel 10:6).

1:15 "Voice like the sound of many waters," like the deafening sound one hears standing at the base of Niagara or Yosemite Falls in springtime (Ezekiel 43:2; Revelation 14:2; 19:6).

1:16 "Seven stars" = angels of the seven churches, 1:20

"A sharp, two-edged sword." The short Roman sword was tongue-like in shape (Morris). It symbolizes irresistible words (2:16; 19:15, 21; Hebrews 4:12; Ephesians 6:17).

1:17-18 "First ... last ... living one." Christ shares the divine attributes (1:4, 8).

"Keys of Death and Hades." Because of Jesus' resurrection, he has now conquered death. He holds the keys, that is, he has authority over it (Matthew 16:19; Isaiah 22:22; Revelation 3:7; 9:1; 20:1).

"Hades" (KJV "hell") is the Greek equivalent of Hebrew "Sheol" and stands for the abode of departed spirits. Here it is not equivalent to Gehenna, the place of torment (Mounce).

Q4. The vision of Christ among the lampstands (1:12-20) is much different than the Carpenter-Teacher who walked the roads of Galilee and Judea. Why? What overall emotions is this vision of Jesus among the lampstands designed to evoke in the reader? Why is this understanding of Jesus important to a balanced faith?
http://www.joyfulheart.com/forums/index.php?showtopic=110

Q5. What is the significance of the exalted Jesus walking among the lampstands? What does this teach us about the church? What does it teach us about Jesus?
http://www.joyfulheart.com/forums/index.php?showtopic=111

Prayer

Lord Jesus, sometimes I find myself taking you for granted. Sometimes I think about you more as a buddy than the awesome, exalted King of the Universe. Please adjust my thinking – not that I would withdraw from you in fear, but that I might be filled with the awe that is appropriate to a revelation of your full glory. In your holy name, I pray. Amen.

2. Letters to the Seven Churches (chapters 2-3)

As you study chapters 2 and 3, I encourage you to print this lesson as well as the two-page comparison chart from Appendix 2 and tape it together. Then in each section, take brief notes in pen or pencil as you read the message to each of the churches. This is the best way to get an understanding of the power of this passage and its message to the church today. The structure of this section is pretty clear. Though messages to some churches may omit one of these, most contain:

1. Portrayal of Jesus
2. Praise for the Church
3. Criticism of the Church
4. Exhortation
5. Correction/Encouragement
6. Penalty/Reward
7. Promises to Overcomers
8. General Admonition

Incidentally, occasionally you run across an interpretation that compares each of the churches to different ages in the life of the church, the last one – the Laodicean church – being the present age. There is absolutely no basis in scripture for this teaching, though it was found in the footnotes of popular study Bibles for years. The danger of this unsubstantiated teaching is that you will gloss over important lessons derived from the other churches. All these lessons are important if the Church today is to become the Church that Jesus can be proud of.

The Church in Ephesus (2:1-7)

2:1 "To the angel." The angels of the seven churches could be:

1. **Guardian angels**, representing the churches (Alford; see Daniel 10:13; 20:21; Matthew 10:18, Acts 12:15).

2. The **pastors** of those churches (Greek *angelos*, messengers; see Matthew 11:10; Hendriksen).

2. Letters to the Seven Churches (chapters 2-3)

3. A personification of the **prevailing spirit** of the church (Mounce, Swete, Morris).

"Him who holds the seven stars in his right hand ... walks in the midst." Christ has the leaders/angels of the churches in his control; He is present in their midst and aware of their activities (Leviticus 26:11-12).

"Ephesus" is the most important city of Asia Minor in the late First Century, at the mouth of the Cayster River, an important commercial and export center for Asia. Chartered as a free city by Rome. Contained temples to three Roman emperors. The Temple of Artemis (Diana) was four times the size of the Parthenon of Athens and considered one of the seven wonders of the ancient world. Famous Christians who lived and ministered there include Aquila and Priscilla, Paul (Acts 19:8-10), Timothy (1 Timothy 1:3), and the Apostle John (Eusebius, *Church History* 5.8.4).

2:4 "Abandoned the love you had at first." A discerning but cold orthodoxy (verse 2) had replaced the fervent, contagious love which once characterized the church (Matthew 24:12-14).

2:5 "Remove your lampstand." If the church turns inward and forsakes its light-bearing responsibility, then Christ removes it ("your lampstand") from the community. See Isaiah 42:6-7; 49:6.

Q1. How can a local congregation lose its "first love" for Jesus? What are the signs of genuine love for Jesus in worship and ministry? How does the lack of love show up? How can a congregation regain this love?
http://www.joyfulheart.com/forums/index.php?showtopic=112

2:6 "Nicolaitans" were a sect in the church that led Christians to compromise the holy standards of the church by encouraging involvement with the idolatry and sexual immorality (2:6, 15, 20-21) that was prevalent in the idolatrous culture of Ephesus and surrounding pagan cities.

2:7 "To him who conquers" (NIV "overcomes"). The Greek verb *nikaō*, means "to win in the face of obstacles, be victor, conquer, overcome, prevail" (BDAG 673). We resist and stand successfully against Satan's temptations by our faith. This word is used a number of times in Revelation. How is a Christian able to overcome according to the following verses?

John 16:33

Romans 12:21

1 John 4:4

1 John 5:4-5

Revelation 12:11

Revelation 15:2

Contrast the "overcomers" with others in Revelation 21:7-8:

"Eat of the tree of life ... in the paradise of God." "Paradise" comes from a Persian word for a "pleasure garden or park." See Genesis 2:9, 15; 3:22-24; and Revelation 22:2. Paradise symbolizes the final state in which God and man are restored to that perfect fellowship which existed in the Garden of Eden before the entrance of sin into the world. Eating the fruit is symbolic of eternal life (Genesis 3:22).

The Church in Smyrna (2:8-11)

2:8 **"Smyrna"** is the only one of the seven cities still lived in – modern Izmir. This beautiful, proud city was larger than Ephesus, with a population of about 200,000. Its strong allegiance to Rome resulted in great persecution for Christians. In Smyrna, Bishop Polycarp was burned at the stake for his faith in 155 AD.

2:9 **"A synagogue of Satan"** describes a religious community that consisted of only outward Jews, not true followers of the Lord. In fact they served their father the devil (John 8:44) who led them to destroy God's true people.

"Poverty." Smyrna and Philadelphia are the only churches for which Jesus offers praise unmixed with criticism. Both see themselves as small and weak – "poverty" (2:9), "little strength" (3:8) – yet Jesus recognizes their true strength.

2:10 "Be faithful ..." captures the theme of Revelation in two words.

"A crown of life" recalls the garland wreath awarded to the victor in the games. See James 1:12; 2 Timothy 4:8. Though the believer may be martyred, his prize is eternal life, not the second death (Revelation 20:6, 14; 21:8), that is, eternal punishment.

The Church in Pergamum (2:12-17)

2:12 "Pergamum" was at one time the capital city of Asia, built atop a 1000-foot cone-shaped hill. It was a center of worship of the pagan gods Zeus, Athene, Dionysis, and Asklepios. In 29 BC, the first temple dedicated to a living emperor was built there.

"Satan's throne" is probably a reference to emperor worship. "As Rome became the center of Satan's activity in the West (13:2; 16:10), so Pergamum had become his 'throne' in the East" (Mounce).

2:14 "The teaching of Balaam." See Numbers 25:1-3 with Numbers 31:15-16. Balaam's sin involved encouraging the Midianite women to seduce the Israelites into idolatry. Balaam is the prototype of corrupt teachers who betray their listeners into fatal compromise with worldly ideologies (Mounce).

Q2. Why would loosening of sexual standards to conform to the prevailing morals of the culture be destructive of vital Christian faith and witness? How has your culture tended to take the edge off your own Christian moral convictions or forced you to be quiet about them?
http://www.joyfulheart.com/forums/index.php?showtopic=113

2:17 "The hidden manna." See Exodus 16:32-34; Hebrews 9:4. The overcomers will partake of the manna hidden in the heavenly temple (11:19).

The Church in Thyatira (2:18-29)

2:18 "Thyatira" was a center for manufacture and marketing, the home of Paul's benefactor Lydia, who was a seller of purple goods (Acts 16:14). Thyatira's numerous trade guilds were inseparably entwined with pagan religious observances posing a special problem for both the spiritual and economic well-being of Christians (Mounce).

"Eyes like a flame of fire" suggest penetrating power to see through Jezebel's seductive teachings, while **"feet like burnished bronze"** conveys the idea of strength and splendor.

2:20 **"Jezebel"** is described here as "that Jezebel of a woman" because her compromise with paganism (2:14) placed her in the succession of the Old Testament Jezebel (1 Kings 16:29-33 and 2 Kings 9:30-37), whose Baal cult was marked by idolatry and ritual prostitution (Bruce). Her teachings tempted Christians to accommodate to heathen practices in the trade guilds. Refusal to conform to the guild practices could mean social isolation and economic hardship. Contrast Jezebel and her followers to "the elect lady and her children" (2 John 1).

Q3. Why do you think the religious compromise required by participating in heathen religious practices in the trade guilds was so spiritually destructive? What compromises do twenty-first century Christians struggle with? Let's not settle for trite legalisms about drinking and smoking. What are the real compromises that dilute vital Christianity?
http://www.joyfulheart.com/forums/index.php?showtopic=114

2:22 **"Those who commit adultery with her...."** John is probably using adultery here as a symbol for religious compromise, rather than implying literal adultery. See James 4:4.

2:26 **"Power over the nations."** Believers shall share rule with the Messiah (5:10; see Psalm 2:8-9).

"The morning star." Probably a reference to the presence of the Lord (22:16; see also Isaiah 14:12; Daniel 12:3).

The Church in Sardis (3:1-6)

3:1 **"Sardis,"** once a powerful city, had declined greatly by the time John was writing. Yet it was still rich and famous, lying at the western end of a great caravan route from Susa in Mesopotamia. The Sardis church receives the most severe denunciation of the seven; it was "a perfect model of inoffensive Christianity" (Caird). The majority had so fully compromised with the pagan environment that the church was Christian in name only (that is, "nominally" Christian).

2. Letters to the Seven Churches (chapters 2-3)

List the four imperatives or commands in 3:2-3

    1.

    2.

    3.

    4.

What might repentance consist of for this church?

3:4 "Soiled their garments." Inscriptions in Asia Minor indicate that soiled clothes disqualified the worshipper and dishonored the god.

3:5 "White garments." See 3:18; 4:4; 6:11; 7:9, 13; 19:14. Portrays justification by Christ (7:13) which fits us for heaven.

"Not blotted out of the book of life." See Exodus 32:32-33; Psalm 69:28; Daniel 12:1. When a criminal's name was removed from the civic register of an Asiatic town, he lost his citizenship.

"Confess his name." See Matthew 10:32-33 and 10:21-22.

The Church in Philadelphia (3:7-13)

3:7 "Philadelphia" (modern Alashehir) is named by the Greek word for "brotherly love." On a major trade route, its economy was based on agriculture and industry. It was remarkable for its many temples and religious festivals, with the worship of Dionysis as its chief pagan cult. Earthquakes had often devastated the city.

"He who has the key of David." See Isaiah 22:15-25 and Rev 1:18. Christ has absolute power to control entrance to eternal life.

3:8 "An open door." No matter if the door to the synagogue has been closed; the door to the messianic kingdom remains open. However in light of Acts 14:27; 1 Corinthians 16:9; 2 Corinthians 2:12; Colossians 4:3; he may be referring to a greater opportunity to be witnesses in their city.

3:9 "Who say they are Jews but are not." See notes on 2:9 above. The church is now the "Israel of God" (Galatians 6:16). See also Isaiah 2:3; 45:14; 49:23; Zechariah 8:20-23.

3:10 "Those who dwell upon the earth" refers consistently in Revelation to the enemies of God's people, not to the church. See 6:10; 8:13; 11:10; 13:8, 14; 17:8.

"I will keep you from the hour of trial...." Pre-tribulation interpreters see this verse as implying "the rapture of the church before the time of trouble referred to as the great tribulation" (Walvoord). But rather than removal from trial, the emphasis here and elsewhere in Revelation is on keeping, preservation, spiritual protection (John 17:15; Revelation 6:9-11; 7:1-3, 14; 12:6).

3:12 "Make him a pillar in the temple," conveys the idea of stability and permanence (see Galatians 2:9; 1 Timothy 3:15). Though the context is the new Jerusalem, the imagery is not the same as seen in 21:22. We must get used to Revelation's fluid imagery. In a city where earthquakes were common, this permanence would be particularly comforting.

The Church in Laodicea (3:14-22)

3:14 "Laodicea" (modern Eski-hisar) was the wealthiest city in Phrygia. The area was famous for manufacture of clothing from soft, glossy black wool, a banking industry, and a medical school. One of its best known medicines was an eye salve made from "Phrygian powder" mixed with oil.

"Amen" is a transliteration of the Hebrew verb *'aman*, "to confirm, support, be faithful" (TWOT 1:51). See Isaiah 65:16 ("the God of the Amen") and 2 Corinthians 1:20. "Amen" expresses "strong affirmation of what is stated" (BDAG 53-54), the acknowledgement of that which is valid and binding.

"Faithful and true witness" reminds Christians that Jesus declared truth in spite of persecution and is our example of a faithful witness in the face of danger and pressure to compromise.

"The beginning of God's creation" (Colossians 1:15-18 and John 1:3). The Greek noun *archē* can mean "one with whom a process begins, beginning" (KJV, NRSV) or "ruler, authority" (NIV; BDAG 137-138). Jesus is the beginner of the new people of God, the Christian community, the New Jerusalem, etc.

3:15 "Neither cold nor hot." Two possible interpretations:

1. Most common is hot = fervent in faith; cold = openly antagonistic (Morris, Ladd, Alford). But why would Christ prefer cold to lukewarm?
2. Perhaps this is a reference to local conditions. Laodicea's water supply, drawn from the hot springs to the south, was still lukewarm after flowing for 5 miles in stone pipes – unlike the cold water which refreshed their neighbors at Colossae,

In any case, Christ is disgusted by the church's nauseating indifference, nominal profession, materialistic complacency.

Q4. Why are so many churches a "hotbed of apathy"? (Don't rag on other denominations!) How can we combat spiritual apathy and an insipid witness in ourselves?
http://www.joyfulheart.com/forums/index.php?showtopic=115

3:18 Christ's counsel is for the church to recognize its need and turn to Him for help. It alludes to the city's famed banking, clothing, and medicine industries.

3:20 "Behold, I stand at the door and knock." Here, speaking to self-sufficient nominal Christians, Christ requests permission to enter and re-establish fellowship.

"Eat with him." In Oriental lands the sharing of a common meal indicates a strong bond of affection and companionship, and becomes a symbol of the intimacy to be enjoyed in the coming messianic kingdom (see Luke 22:30; Revelation 19:9).

These letters are intended as a particular encouragement to real churches at a specific point of their histories. However, they serve as a warning, comfort, and promise to churches with similar characteristics in our own day.

Q5. Summarize the lessons of this chapter. What are the churches criticized for? What are they praised for? How should these observations shape the twenty-first century Church?
http://www.joyfulheart.com/forums/index.php?showtopic=116

Prayer

Jesus, Lord of the Church and Ruler of all, forgive us for the sin and apathy we find in ourselves and in our churches. Teach us how to repent – not with knee-jerk legalism, but with a zeal based on love for you. In your holy name, we pray. Amen.

3. The Lion That Is the Lamb (chapters 4-5)

We've seen the glorified Christ speaking to his Church in Revelation 2-3. Now the scene shifts and we see the glory of Almighty God as well as the worthiness of the Lamb of God. We are also introduced to the worship that goes on before the throne of God. Too often we are bored by worship, but worship is our destiny and our privilege as God's people.

Detail of "Adoration of the Lamb" from the Ghent Altarpiece (1427-1430), by Hubert and Jan van Eyck, Cathedral of St. Bavo, Ghent, The Netherlands.

4:2 "Behold, a throne." Heavens and earth are not ruled by Satan but by the throne of God. "We know the one who holds the future." See Psalm 47:8; 1 Kings 22:19; Isaiah 6:1-8; Ezekiel 1:26-28; Daniel 7:9-10.

4:4 "Twenty-four elders." Twenty four seems to symbolize the 12 patriarchs (the people of God in OT days) and the 12 apostles (the people of God in NT days), thus the whole church of God, both before and since the time of Christ (Revelation 21:12-14). We, too, are seated in heavenly places with Christ (Ephesians 2:6) and share his reign (Revelation 5:10).

4:6 "Four living creatures." These angelic beings are related to the four-faced cherubim of Ezekiel 1 and 10 with some differences. (See also Isaiah 6:2-3.) They serve as spokesman (Revelation 6:1, 3, 5, 7) and are continually singing and praising God (4:8). Winged creatures are commonly found in Near Eastern archeology, such as the griffin. Four seems to be another number of completeness, especially concerning universal or worldwide scope, the created world (Beale 59, Wilcock), the four corners of the earth, the four winds (7:1).

3. The Lion That Is the Lamb (chapters 4-5)

Q1. Many Christian hymns, songs, and choruses come from Revelation chapters 4 and 5. Which can you think of?
http://www.joyfulheart.com/forums/index.php?showtopic=118

4:10 "Fall down and worship." The word "worship," Greek *proskuneō*, originally involved the idea of prostrating oneself before deity to kiss his feet or the hem of his garment.

"Lay their crowns before the throne," symbolically acknowledging that their authority is a delegated authority.

Winged lion with ram's head and griffin's hind legs, enameled tile frieze from the palace of Darius I at Susa, c. 510 BC, Louvre, Paris.

Q2. These chapters contain many insights into worship that have been adopted by the Christian Church. What do you learn about Christian worship from chapters 4 and 5? Don't miss the basics. Your list might include 20 elements and concepts of worship – or more.
http://www.joyfulheart.com/forums/index.php?showtopic=119

5:1 "A scroll written within and on the back." Probably it represents God's eternal plan with respect to the entire universe throughout history, and concerning all creatures in all ages and unto all eternity. Hence it is full of writing on both sides. The seven seals signify the absolute inviolability of the scroll. (See Daniel 8:26; Isaiah 29:11).

5:2 "Who is worthy?" The call is for someone who is worthy to perform the supreme service of bringing history to its consummation.

5:4 "I wept much" at the prospect of an indefinite postponement of God's final and decisive action.

5:5 "The Lion of the tribe of Judah," Genesis 49:9-10.

"The Root of David (Isaiah 11:1; Romans 15:12) **has conquered"** – victory through complete self-sacrifice. Jesus, of course, is the descendent of David (son of Jesse), and heir to David's kingdom – the coming Messiah to whom the prophecies look forward.

Albrecht Dürer, "Adoration of the Lamb" (1498), woodcut.

5:6 "A Lamb standing as though it had been slain," Greek *sphazō*, literally "butcher or murder someone" (BDAG 979). This word also describes the fate of Christ's followers (6:9). On Jesus as the Lamb, see John 1:29; Isaiah 53:7.

"Seven horns and seven eyes." Seven = perfection, completeness. Horn = power. Eyes = wisdom, seeing, perception.

5:8 "A harp" (Psalm 33:2-3) and **"incense"** (Deuteronomy 33:10; Psalm 141:2; Revelation 8:3) typify our prayers that rise before God's throne.

5:9 "By your blood did you ransom men for God" (1 Corinthians 6:20; 1 Peter 1:18-19; Revelation 14:4).

Q3. (Revelation 5:9, 12) *What made Jesus so worthy* of opening the scroll and thus bringing history to its consummation? Why was this act so noteworthy and praiseworthy?
http://www.joyfulheart.com/forums/index.php?showtopic=120

5:10 "A kingdom and priests to our God." A fulfillment of Exodus 19:6 (see also 1 Peter 2:5, 9). Corporately believers are a kingdom. Individually we are priests to God.

"They shall reign," sharing Christ's rule (2:26-27).

"On earth." When this reign takes place isn't entirely clear – either during the millennium (20:4) or the "new heavens and new earth" (22:5). Whichever it is, the destiny of believers is bound up with planet earth. Since our resurrection bodies will be like Christ's (Philippians 3:21; 1 John 3:2), we will have the ability to operate in both spiritual and physical realms.

Q4. (Revelation 5:10) How can our destiny as believers include reigning? In what sense could we reign? In what sense do we serve as priests? In what sense are we a kingdom?
http://www.joyfulheart.com/forums/index.php?showtopic=121

Q5. (Revelation 5:13) What is the significance of the same quality of worship being offered to both God the Father and Jesus Christ the Son? What does this tell us about their relationship to each other? Their relationship to us?
http://www.joyfulheart.com/forums/index.php?showtopic=122

Prayer

Father, we tend to be so self-centered. Teach us to center our lives on you and your son Jesus Christ, to get our priorities straight, and to live lives of worship. In Jesus' name, we pray. Amen.

4. The 144,000 (chapters 6-10)

The writer of Revelation shows God's judgments in the Last Days unfolding in three series of seven. Whether these are sequential and chronological, we can't know for sure. It may be helpful to see at least some of these as parallel with each other. To see the parallels, see the Parallelism in Revelation chart in Appendix 2.

1. Seven Seals (6:1-8:5)
2. Seven Trumpets (8:6-11:19)
3. Seven Bowls of Wrath (15:7-16:21)

In the midst of this awesome destruction we see the faithful and witnessing church, herself protected from God's judgments (7:3), but subject to intense persecution and martyrdom by the enraged enemies of God (6:9-11; 7:14; 11:3; 12:11, 17; 13:7).

Albrecht Dürer, "Four Horsemen of the Apocalypse" (1497-98), woodcut, 11x15"

Lesson 4 is a long one, made up of five chapters from Revelation. There's a lot of material here, but what I'm focusing on are the general outlines of God's judgments upon the earth and particularly the believers who are on earth and in heaven during this time of judgment and intense persecution.

At this point in Revelation, debates about the identity of various groups get hot and heavy. My goal isn't to convince you of a particular view, but to help you understand the core message of the Book of Revelation. The discussion questions you find in this lesson aren't meant to get you to take sides in a speculative doctrinal debate, but to reflect on what the text teaches us – in particular, lessons that we can apply in our own lives.

You'll find charts for this lesson of the Seven Seals, Seven Trumpets, and Parallelism. As you study these chapters of Revelation, take notes on these charts to help you grasp what is going on. You can use print out these charts on your printer, linked to

www.jesuswalk.com/revelation/revelation-lesson-handouts.pdf

The Seven Seals (6:1-17)

The **seven seals** begin with the "Four Horsemen of the Apocalypse", the subject of Albrecht Dürer's famous woodcut. The imagery is similar to Zechariah 1:8-15; 6:1-8, with content that is similar to Ezekiel 14:12-23 and Leviticus 26:18-28. The parallels with Matthew 24 and Luke 21:9-27 are interesting if not complete. (See the Parallelism Chart in Appendix.2) The destruction of Jerusalem (70 AD) is omitted in Revelation, since it had presumably already occurred by the time the vision was recorded about 95 AD. If you haven't already, why don't you print out the 7 Seals chart found in Appendix 2 on which you can take notes.

6:1 "A white horse ... bow ... crown conquering and to conquer." The identity of the white horse and rider is disputed.

1. **The rider is Christ, the white horse, the victorious progress of the gospel**, in accordance with 19:11; 5:5, Matthew 10:34; 24:14; Mark 13:10, Psalm 45: 3-5. White is used elsewhere in Revelation in a good sense (14 times).
2. But others insist that **the four horses belong together**. A horse is symbolic of strength, terror, warfare, and conquest (Isaiah 30:16; 31:1-3; Job 39:22-25). The first rider would then represent military conquest. The bow is a symbol of military power (Hosea 1:5; Jeremiah 51:56; Isaiah 41:2). (So Mounce, Morris, Bruce, Beasley-Murray, Beale). This view makes the most sense to me.

6:3 "Horse, bright red ... take peace away from the earth" (Matthew 24:6-7; 2 Thessalonians 2:6; Zechariah 14:13; Isaiah 19:2).

4. The 144,000 (chapters 6-10)

6:5 "A black horse ... a balance is his hand." The balance indicates a time of scarcity when food is measured out at greatly inflated prices. A denarius was about one day's wage, for which a man could buy enough wheat for himself only, or less nutritious food for his family, inflated to 10 times the normal price. Since the roots of the olive and vine go deeper, they would not be affected by a limited drought which would nearly destroy the grain crop.

6:7 "A pale horse ... Death, and Hades followed him." This horse was the color of a corpse. Death is brought by the "four sore acts of judgment" of Ezekiel 14:21. Three cycles of judgment seem to appear in increasing intensity: (1) The fourth **seal** affects "a fourth part of the earth" (6:8), (2) the **trumpets** destroy a third (8:7,8,10,12), and (3) the destruction by the **bowls** is complete and final (chapter 16).

6:9 "I saw under the altar the souls ... slain for the word of God." Christian persecution and martyrdom is inevitable in the end times and is seen as a sacrifice to God, as represented by their location "under the altar" (see 2 Timothy 4:6; Philippians 2:17). Notice the mention of **"the testimony they had maintained,"** part of a theme throughout Revelation encouraging to the church to continue its faithful witness in spite of persecution and death (See the notes on 1:2.).

6:10 Vindication and justice, not revenge, is the theme of their prayer. See Psalm 79:10; Habakkuk 1:2.

6:12 "The sixth seal ... earthquake," etc. See Isaiah 2:10, 19, 21. Haggai 2:6; Joel 2:30-31 quoted in Acts 2:19-20; Isaiah 34:4. The heavens are removed like an unrolled papyrus scroll, which, if it broke in the middle, would roll quickly back on either side (Mounce).

6:16 "What sinners dread most is not death, but the revealed Presence of God" (Swete). Better death by a crushing avalanche than face the wrath of the Lamb.

If we identify the sixth seal with Matthew 24:29, it would be placed "immediately after the tribulation" and just before the public coming of the Son of Man, accompanied by the "mourning" of all the tribes of the earth, that is, the unbelievers. That assumes, however, that both Revelation and Matthew follow the same time-based chronology.

Q1. (Revelation 6) Who initiates this great storm of destruction represented by the Seven Seals? Against whom is it directed? Is it just?
http://www.joyfulheart.com/forums/index.php?showtopic=123

Q2. (Revelation 6:9-11) What do we learn about the Church from what is revealed in the Fifth Seal? Where are these "souls" at the time of this scene? What does their proximity to the altar signify? Why were they killed? Why do they ask for vengeance? Is that a Christian prayer? What does the white robe represent? What do we learn from their instruction to "wait a little longer"?

http://www.joyfulheart.com/forums/index.php?showtopic=124

The 144,000 (7:1-8)

Chapter 7 This chapter is an interlude between the sixth and seventh seals. The purpose is to assure the Church that she shall be protected from the wrath of God upon the world.

7:1 Four is again seen as the number of the created world – four corners of the earth, four winds.

7:2 "The seal of the living God." The idea of the seal comes from signet rings like those used by Oriental kings to authenticate and protect official documents, and to declare their ownership (22:3-4). The imagery is from Ezekiel 9 where a man with an inkhorn places an X or a + on the forehead of the faithful remnant in Jerusalem to protect them from God's judgments upon the city. The idea may go back to the mark of the Passover Lamb's blood upon a house that protected the Israelites within during God's judgment on the Egyptians (Exodus 12). The seal in Revelation is the name of the Lamb and his Father (14:1). They are preserved from the wrath of God (1 Thessalonians 5:9), though apparently not from persecution (see 20:4) nor the effects of the destruction being wreaked upon the earth. The seal provides spiritual protection for Christians against the power of satanic forces and is emblematic of salvation (2 Timothy 2:19; 2 Corinthians 1:22; Ephesians 1:13; 4:30). This seal contrasts with the mark of the beast (13:16; 14:9, 16:2; 19:20; 20:4).

7:3 Revelation offers **two views at the 144,000**.

1. 7:3-8 shows them **on earth**, protected from God's wrath and Satan's trickery by the "seal" on their foreheads.

2. 14:1-5 views them **in heaven** before the throne, now "redeemed from the earth." It makes sense to assume that these 144,000 comprise the same group in both places.

"144, 000 ... out of every tribe of the sons of Israel." There are 12 tribes listed, but Dan is omitted in favor of Manasseh who is included in addition to Joseph (see Genesis 35:22-26). The number 144,000 is 12 squared and multiplied by 1000. One thousand was for Greek speakers the "big number" like we use the word "a million." Thus 144,000 is a two-fold way of emphasizing completeness – the full number which includes many, many people. I believe that number is not to be taken literally but symbolically, like a great many of the elements of John's vision (see chapter 21, especially verse 17).

Who are the 144,000? Literal Israel? Or the church?

1. **Literal Israel might be the reference.** Romans 11:25-26 indicates a future salvation for Paul's kinsmen, probably after the "times of the Gentiles are fulfilled" (Luke 21:24; so Beasley-Murray 141). Dispensational theology, the Scofield Reference Bible, Hal Lindsey, Walvrood, and others make a clear separation between the Jews and the church in prophecy. They see the rapture of the church as prior to the seven seals, the 144,000 as literal Jews, and the white-robed saints of 7:14 as Gentiles saved by the preaching of the 144,000 witnesses during the tribulation.
2. Jehovah's Witnesses see the **144,000 referring to the true church in the Last Times**, but take the number literally as a reference to members their own sect only. When their numbers grew beyond 144,000, their literal interpretation forced them to emphasize an entirely earth-bound paradise for later-born Jehovah's Witnesses.
3. However, for several reasons, I believe that **the 144,000 should be seen symbolically as the whole Church** (Beale 416-423, Ladd 111-117, Caird 94-96, Mounce 168-170). Here's why I hold this view:

   - The Church can be referred to as the twelve tribes (James 1:1 with 1 Peter 1:1), the Christian as the true Jew (Romans 2:29; Revelation 2:9; 3:9), and as the "Israel of God" (Galatians 6:16). The Church is the heir of the promises and distinctions of Israel (1 Peter 2:9-10; Galatians 3:29; Philippians 3:3; Romans 4:11). The Church has been grafted into the one "olive tree" of God's people while the Jews as a people were broken off (Romans 11:17-21; Matthew 21:43).
   - The "ten lost tribes" of Israel that went into exile have been assimilated into other cultures and lost their identity as Jews.
   - As the number 144,000 is symbolic here, so also the designation "sons of Israel" is probably figurative of the Church.

- All "servants of God" on earth at the time were sealed. Unless the Church has been raptured by this time, these servants must include Gentile Christians. The martyrs of 6:9-11 correspond to the Christians to be persecuted in Mt 24:9-14. The rapture in Matthew 24:29-31 is supposed to come "immediately after the tribulation of those days."
- Protection from the wrath of God is possible for Christians while on the earth. For example, Israel in Egypt was protected from the ten plagues upon the Egyptians. The promise of sealing in Revelation 7:2-4 grants protection as did the sealing in Ezekiel 9.

Q3. (Revelation 7:1-4) There's disagreement about exactly who the 144,000 represent. Let's not debate that, but look deeper. **From 7:1-4 what do we learn about God? Read Ezekiel 9, then answer: What is this seal supposed to do for the 144,000?** (Please wait to consider 14:1-5 until we get there, okay?)
http://www.joyfulheart.com/forums/index.php?showtopic=125

The Great Multitude in White Robes (7:9-17)

7:9 "A great multitude clothed in white robes." Now the scene shifts from the 144,000 who are, at this point, on the earth, to an unnumbered multitude in heaven before the throne of God.

7:9-12 In this throne room scene we hear the same kind of worship we saw in chapters 4 and 5. The white-robed humans praise God for their salvation. Humans, angels, elders, and the four living creatures all bow down to worship and offer a fitting seven-fold doxology before God. Count the seven elements in 7:12.

7:14 "These are they who have come out of the great tribulation." How they came out of the great tribulation is not stated. The possibilities are: (1) by natural death, (2) by martyrdom (in which case they might include members of the group described in 6:9-11), or (3) by rapture (see Matthew 24: 29-31; 1 Thessalonians 4:14-18; alluded to in 1 Corinthians 15:51-52). The chronological order of this scene is not given, only that John saw it after the scene of the 144,000 on earth (7:9). Could it be that these white-robed saints represent the same 144,000 who have gone through the tribulation and are now in heaven, at rest (as in 14:1-5)? We can't be sure.

4. The 144,000 (chapters 6-10)

"The great tribulation" is the "hour of trial" (3:10), the "time of trouble" (Daniel 12:1), and is probably the same times described in Matthew 24:21, 29. The destiny of the saints who follow the Lamb has always been persecution. The great tribulation is that persecution escalated in intensity to fever pitch. This great multitude comes from "all nations," the result of the Great Commission (Matthew 28:19), the great work of preaching "the gospel of the kingdom," which must be completed before the end comes (Matthew 24:14). This great innumerable multitude is probably a picture of the entire church of Christ, gathered in the new heavens and new earth (see 21:1-4).

"Washed their robes ... in the blood of the Lamb." Being washed in blood seems like a strange metaphor, but it is originally seen in Genesis 49:11. The idea of sins being cleansed by the atonement of blood sacrifices is a common figure in the Old Testament and the new (for example, Hebrews 9:14 and 1 John 1:7). This group of forgiven and cleansed people is likely to be the same as the 144,000 as "these (who) have been redeemed from mankind," bought by the atoning blood of the Lamb whom they follow (14:4) and worship (7:10).

7:15-17 The description of their privilege to live in God's presence has inspired hope in hurting and oppressed Christians throughout the centuries. This passage contains a number of echoes from the Prophet Isaiah (4:5-6; 25:4-5, 8; 49:10; also in Revelation 21:4). These verses capture the hope of those who must undergo the pain and hurt of this world order. Notice the deliberate incongruous images of the Lamb who is also a Shepherd (7:17), with strong echoes from the Twenty-Third Psalm!

What are the promises made to this group of Christians who have come out of great tribulation? In the space provided, write down the poetic way in which each of these promises is framed. This is not to share in the Forum, but for your own notes.

Presence of God (7:15a)

Protection of God (7:15b)

Provision of God (7:16)

Guidance of the Lamb (7:17a)

Salvation from the Lamb (7:17b. What does "living water" signify here?)

Comfort from God (7:17c)

Q4. (Revelation 7:9-18). From this passage what do we learn about the kind of people who make up the "great multitude" before the throne? Let's *not* debate whether they are the 144,000 or not. But what is their origin? What does their spirit within them cause them to do? What does the first verse of the song "Amazing Grace" have to do with 7:14?

http://www.joyfulheart.com/forums/index.php?showtopic=126

The Seventh Seal and the Golden Censer (8:1-5)

8:1 "The seventh seal ... silence." Silence is often associated with judgment in the Old Testament (Psalm 115:17; 31:17; Isaiah 47:5; Ezekiel 27:32; Amos 8:2-3; Lamentations 2:10-11; especially Habakkuk 2:20 and Zechariah 2:13; Beale 446-454).

8:3 "A golden censer" is an elegant utensil for burning incense. Incense often gracing the homes of monarchs and the wealthy (Psalm 45:8). In the Bible, however, burning incense is almost always mentioned in the context of worship of a deity. In Revelation, incense is used as a metaphor of prayer (see also 5:8).

The Seven Trumpets (8:6-9:21)

The Israelites used a ram's horn, the shofar, as a trumpet to signal coming events and to coordinate troops in battle. If you haven't already, why don't you print out the 7 Trumpets chart found in Appendix 2 on which you can take notes.

8:6 The seven trumpets seem to develop out of the seventh seal. But do the trumpets follow the seals in chronological succession? There are several views:

1. **That the trumpets follow the seals in chronological succession.** This is the simplest understanding of these verses in the opinion of C. C. Ryrie, Salem Kirban, and other dispensationalist (pre-tribulation, pre-millennial) writers. They see the seven seals as belonging to the first 3-1/2 years of the Tribulation Period; the Trumpets and Bowls to the second 3-1/2 year period of the Tribulation. However, this view has (as does every other view) certain objections which have led to other approaches.

2. **That the trumpets and seals and bowls are at least partly parallel chronologically.** Wilcock fits the visions into the chronological framework of Jesus' Mt. Olivet discourse (Matthew 24) and sees a "repeat of patterns." A major fact which seems to substantiate this parallelism theory is that both the sixth seal and the seventh trumpet seem to declare the events of the coming of Christ, parallel to Matthew 24:29-31. Other writers with various adaptations of this theory are Morris, Ladd, Bruce, Hendriksen, and Beale. This is the view which I consider preferable and most helpful to understanding the intention of the book. Study the Parallelism in Revelation chart in Appendix 2 to see this.

If the church is present, as I believe it to be, during this period (9:4-5), it is certainly sealed and protected from the wrath of God upon the earth, much as the Israelites in Egypt were protected from the plagues (see Exodus 8:22; 9:4, 26; 11:7). However, when final destruction comes, God's servants are removed (for example, Lot in Sodom, Genesis 19:12-13, 22; and Noah and his family, Genesis 6-8).

Notice that some of the trumpets seem to parallel, but with greater intensity, the plagues on Egypt, Exodus 7-11. That only 1/3 of the earth was destroyed indicates the as yet restricted intensity of God's trumpet judgments.

8:7 "First trumpet ... hail and fire ... blood." See the seventh Egyptian plague (Exodus 9:13-35).

8:8 "Second trumpet ... sea became blood." See the first Egyptian plague (Exodus 7:20-21).

8:10 "Third trumpet ... Wormwood" also suggests the pollution of the fresh water experienced in the first Egyptian plague. Wormwood is a plant with a strongly bitter taste. See Proverbs 5:3-4; Lamentations 3:19; Jeremiah 9:15; 23:15.

8:12 "Fourth trumpet ... darkness." Compare the ninth Egyptian plague (Exodus 10:21-23). These last day plagues are the prelude to that great and final exodus in which the church is taken out of the world and enters into the eternal presence of God. See Amos 5:18; Joel 2; Mark 13:24; Isaiah 13:10.

8:13 "Woe, woe, woe." These woes correspond to the last three judgments (9:12; 11:14). The eagle, a predator, now announces the last three parts of the vision.

9:1 "A star fallen from heaven to earth." See Revelation 8:10; Luke 10:18; Isaiah 14:12; Revelation 12:4. However, he may well be the angel of God seen in 20:1.

9:2 "Shaft of the bottomless pit" (Greek *abyssos*). The rising smoke of a great furnace suggests that the abyss is a place of torment of the evil spirits imprisoned there until the final judgment (Luke 8:31; Revelation 20:3; 11:7; 17:8; 9:1, 11; 20:1, 3; also Jude 6; 2 Peter 2:4; Luke 16:23-24).

9:3 "Locusts ... power of scorpions." See the eighth Egyptian plague (Exodus 10:1-20), and the vision of Joel 1:2-2:1. Throughout the Old Testament the locust is a symbol of destruction. Breeding in the desert, they invade cultivated areas in search of food. They may travel in a column 100 feet deep and up to four miles in length, leaving the land stripped bare of all vegetation. The scorpion is a lobster-like vermin, 4 to 5 inches long with a stinger on the end of the tail that secretes a poison when it strikes.

9:11 "The angel of the bottomless pit." This is not likely to be Satan, but a servant of God who controls the pit. Hebrew ***Abaddon***, seen in Job 28:22, is associated with *Sheol*, death. ***Apollyon*** means "the destroyer" in Greek. Destroying angels are seen in God's judgments in Sodom (Genesis 19:13, 22) and Jerusalem (Ezekiel 9:2, 5-8; 1 Chronicles 21:16, 30; 2 Kings 19:35; etc.).

9:13 "Sixth trumpet ... four angels released" at the head of 200 million troops of cavalry.

9:18 "Brimstone" is what is known today as sulfur, a greenish yellow element. See the judgment on Sodom and Gomorrah (Genesis 19:24).

9:20 "Did not repent." The limited scope of these judgments was designed to provoke repentance, yet "those who dwell upon the earth" were set in their wickedness, much as in the days of Noah (Genesis 6:5, 11).

The Angel and the Little Scroll (10:1-11)

10:1 "Another mighty angel." See Ezekiel 1:26-28 for a similar description.

10:3-4 "Seal up what the seven thunders have said." Part of God's plans are yet unrevealed and hidden from God's people. See Daniel 12:4, 9.

10:6 "No more delay" is in contrast to 6:11, "rest a little longer." The opportunity for repentance is gone; God's judgments now move forward to the final consummation without interruption.

10:7 "In the days of the trumpet call ... the seventh." See Revelation 11:15; 1 Corinthians 15:52; 1 Thessalonians 4:16; Matthew 24:31. In other words, this is the period of the very end.

"The mystery of God" refers to the purpose of God's total redemptive plan, which includes the judgment of evil and the eschatological salvation of his people (Ladd).

10:9 "The little scroll ... bitter to your stomach, but sweet as honey in your mouth." See parallel in Ezekiel 2:8-3:3. Beale says, "The little scroll connotes the Christian's purposes on a small scale in imitation of the large-scale purposes of Christ signified by the larger book (scroll) of chapter 5." The sweetness is closeness to God and His Word (Psalm 19:7-11; 119:97-104; Proverbs 16:21-24; 24:13-14; Jeremiah 15:16; Deuteronomy 8:3) as well as the grace of God to the redeemed. The bitterness is disputed:

1. The **ordeal of the church** and of its two witnesses in chapter 11 (Mounce, Alford, Hendriksen, see 6:10, Ezekiel 3:14).
2. **Final judgment** upon the earth's wicked people (Luke 19:41; Jeremiah 9:1; Ladd, Morris, Wilcock, Beale).

Q5. (Revelation 10:1-9) What is bitter about what you've read in Revelation 6 through 10? What is sweet? Why do we tend to reject what is hard for us to understand?
http://www.joyfulheart.com/forums/index.php?showtopic=127

In this week's lesson we have seen a panorama of terrible judgment and destruction:

1. The Seven Seals (chapter 6).
2. The sealing of the 144,000, which is symbolic of the whole Church, to protect them both from God's wrath and Satan's fury (7:1-8).
3. A scene change to the heavenly throne room where the saved of earth – now come out of the "great tribulation" of the last days – are standing before the throne of God and the Lamb in worship (7:9-17).
4. The Seven Trumpets (chapters 8-9) which bring even greater judgments upon the earth.
5. The Little Scroll, both sweet and bitter (chapter 10).

Even though the Seventh Trumpet doesn't sound until the end of chapter 11, I am ending this long lesson with chapter 10. Chapters 11-13 talk about the role of the Church during this time of intense persecution, so I want to consider them together in the next lesson.

The events of this chapter are difficult. You may sense the bitterness of the heavy punishment on those with unrepentant hearts (9:20-21). Yet we can be encouraged by the fact that none of these things shall move the Church. We are watched out for and protected by God in the worst of times, and have a hope of joy in the presence of the Lamb. The message of Revelation is both sweet and bitter. Come soon, Lord Jesus.

Prayer

Lord, my soul cries out when I read of all this destruction. Why, Lord, why? I understand your forgiveness, but not your judgment. What can forestall your judgment? What can I do to help those in danger of judgment? How can I prepare to be alive during this great tribulation if that is your plan for me? Thank you for your promise of aid and protection in the darkest hour. In Jesus' name I trust. Amen.

5. By the Blood of the Lamb (chapters 11-13)

Now we're in the thick of interpreting Revelation. In this lesson we'll be considering:

1. The identity of the Two Witnesses
2. The nature of the Great Tribulation
3. What Temple may be present during the Last Days
4. The Woman and Male Child
5. The Dragon, the Antichrist, and the False Prophet

They're all in these passages. We won't agree on all these identifications, I'm sure. But I hope you'll learn something that makes sense to you in the context of the entire Book of Revelation.

Fortunately, the important questions of this section are not "Who is the Antichrist?" or "Will there be a literal temple?" The

English painter William Blake (1757-1827) was commissioned to illustrate the Book of Revelation. Here is his "The Great Red Dragon and the Woman Clothed with the Sun" (c. 1805), National Gallery of Art, Washington, DC).

real message has to do with being faithful witnesses, even when faced with death. That's what the early church has to teach us twenty-first century Christians who can be silenced with the sneer of peer pressure. We need to learn how to be faithful witnesses to death, so watch as this theme is developed.

The Two Witnesses (11:1-14)

Chapter 11 is difficult to interpret with certainty. There are two popular of views:

1. Dispensationalists take the symbols in a **literal manner**: the temple will actually exist, the two witnesses are two individuals, and the altar will be placed where ancient sacrifices are renewed (Walvoord, Ryrie). This is possible. However, there are elements in this vision which cannot be interpreted literally and demand a symbolic interpretation.
2. For this reason, most scholars take this vision as **symbolic**. I believe that this passage outlines the function of the **witnessing church**. Its lot will be hard, but eventual triumph is sure.

11:1 "Measure." see Ezekiel 40:3; 42:20; Zechariah 2:1-5. A symbol of separating the holy from the common, and therefore protecting from evil. This is the same function of "sealing" in Revelation 7.

"Temple of God" is symbolic for the church, God's people, the true Israel (see 1 Corinthians 3:16; 2 Corinthians 6:16-17; Ephesians 2:19-21; 1 Peter 2:5).

11:2 "Court outside the temple," that is, the "Court of the Gentiles," probably represents those who are not the true Israel, perhaps those who are outwardly Christians but not true believers or the unbelieving "Gentile" world.

"Given over to the nations ... for forty-two months." Compare "the times of the Gentiles" (Luke 21:24). The 42 months = 3-1/2 years = 1260 days = "time, times, and half a time." This period of time comes from the prophecy in Daniel 9:24-27. The last week of Daniel's "70 weeks of years" occurs after "an anointed one shall be cut off" (Daniel 9:26), that is, the Messiah is crucified. The final "seven year" period is not literal time, I believe, but symbolic of the "gospel age" and is characterized by the proclamation of the gospel, which includes a period of terrible persecution ("great tribulation") at the very end. (See Revelation 11:2-3; 12:6, 14; 13:5; Daniel 7:25; 9:27; 12:11.) Even though each is referred to as "3-1/2 years," I don't expect them to be the same length in chronological time. Here's how I analyze these two confusing "3-1/2 year" periods:

Gospel Age ("Tribulation")	"Great Tribulation"
Church trampled 42 months, 2 witnesses prophecy 1260 days (Revelation 11:2-3)	2 witnesses dead, 3-1/2 days (Revelation 11:9)
Woman in wilderness, church protected to declare gospel, 1260 days. 1X, 2X 1/2X (Revelation 12:6, 14)	War on offspring; beast: authority; church decimated by persecution, 42 months (Revelation 13:5-7)
Mystery of lawlessness at work but restrained (2 Thessalonians 2:7)	The lawless one will be revealed (2 Thessalonians 2:8)
Spirit of antichrist (1 John 2:18b)	Antichrist prevails (1 John 2:18a)
Sacrifice and offering (Daniel 9:27a)	Abomination in temple, desolator (Daniel 9:27b)
Power of holy people (Daniel 12:7a; 1X, 2X, 1/2X).	After shattering of power of holy people. Time after abomination, 1290 days. Total = 1335 days (Daniel 12:7b, 11-12)
	"Little Horn" wears out saints 1X, 2X 1/2X (Daniel 7:21-25)

11:3-4 "Two witnesses." Many identifications have been suggested. I believe they represent the witnessing Church throughout the Gospel Age.

"Two olive trees" (see Zechariah 4:1-14) are symbolic of the oil (Zechariah 4:12) and of the Spirit (Zechariah 4:6) who provides oil to maintain the **"two lampstands"** (see Revelation 1:20).

So who are these two witnesses? Some think they may be the two faithful witnessing churches of Asia – Smyrna and Philadelphia. Others see Elijah and Moses. I've heard Billy Graham and Oral Roberts mentioned. But I believe these two witnesses represent the whole witnessing Church. The testimony of at least two witnesses was considered credible in Jewish law. I think the two witnesses indicate the adequacy and credibility of the Church's testimony (Deuteronomy 17:6; 19:15; Numbers 35:30).

11:5-6 The Church's power over rain and plagues typify Elijah and Moses (prophets and law). The Church's power is considerable (Matthew 16:18-19; 18:18-20; Luke 10:19).

11:7 "The beast that comes up from the Abyss" is of Satanic origin and represents the Antichrist. This is the first of about 35 references in Revelation to the "beast." The term "antichrist" is not used in the Book of Revelation, but only in 1 John 2:18, 22; 4:3; 2 John 7. However, the concept occurs elsewhere, particularly as the "Man of Lawlessness" in 2 Thessalonians 2:1-12. He leads a rebellion against God and usurps the place of God, demanding worship. In addition, he performs various signs and wonders (Mark 13:6, 21-22). There is some speculation that the beasts of Revelation picture the Roman system with its "divine" emperor and emperor worship (Duane F. Watson, "Antichrist," DLNT 50-53).

11:8 "Will make war ... conquer them ... and kill them." See Revelation 12:17; 2 Thessalonians 2:3-4, 8-10; Daniel 7:21. This is the reign of the Antichrist and the decimation of the church by martyrdom. However, if the **"two witnesses"** represent two of the seven churches of Asia, then it may indicate that only part of the church is martyred. We know that there will be at least a few Christians left on the earth when Christ comes (Luke 18:8; 1 Corinthians 15:51; etc.). "Night comes when no one can work" (John 9:4).

11:8 "The great city." Some feel this refers to literal Jerusalem **"where their Lord was crucified."** Others feel this is a reference to "the world" in general, represented by "the great city, Babylon" in Revelation 16 to 18.

11:9 "Three days and a half," a short period compared to the ascendancy of the church for 3-1/2 years = 1260 days.

11:11-13 "Come up here." Resurrection and rapture are depicted. See 1 Corinthians 15:51-57; 1 Thessalonians 4:15-17; Matthew 24:31; Mark 13:26-27.

Q1. (11:3-12) Interpreters disagree upon the identity of the Two Witnesses, but they are certainly strong and brave. What positive characteristics do you see in their actions that we should emulate in our day? What is their reward?
http://www.joyfulheart.com/forums/index.php?showtopic=128

The Seventh Trumpet (11:15-19)

11:15 **"Seventh trumpet."** This is the last trumpet (see references in my notes under 10:7). Finally, Christ rules on earth and sets up his eternal Messianic kingdom: "The kingdom of the world has become the kingdom of our Lord and of his Christ, and he will reign for ever and ever." Hallelujah!

11:18 Now comes the time for **"the dead to be judged"** and **"for rewarding thy servants."** This corresponds to the "great white throne judgment" (Revelation 20:11-14) and the "judgment seat of Christ" (2 Corinthians 5:10; Romans 14:10).

The Woman and the Dragon (12:1-13:1a)

Chapter 12 marks a major division. One of the central themes of Revelation is the spiritual warfare between the Kingdom of God and the kingdom of Satan. In this vision, war in heaven is pictured in "mythological colors" (Ladd) between a great red dragon and a heavenly woman.

The Church's true adversary is revealed. Cast down from heaven, knowing that his time is short, Satan turns in his rage to destroy Christ's Church. Knowing that this is the death struggle of a defeated foe, the Church is strengthened in her resolve to hold fast and to conquer.

12:1 **"A woman"** represents the whole family of Israel out of which the Messiah is born. She is in fact the Church: the old Israel and the new Israel. See Psalm 104:2; Genesis 37:9; Isaiah 26:17-18. The **"moon under her feet"** = dominion, the **"crown"** = royalty.

12:3 **"A great red dragon"** = "that ancient serpent, who is called the Devil and Satan" (verse 9). The **"seven heads"** may depict the completeness or universality of his usurped sovereignty. The **"ten horns"** = power, might (see Daniel 7:7, 24) and are later seen to represent ten kings (Revelation 13:1; 17:12).

12:4 **"His tail swept down a third of the stars of heaven and cast them to earth."** See Daniel 8:10; 2 Peter 2:4; Jude 6; Isaiah 14:12; Matthew 25:41; Revelation 12:7-9. Does this refer to fallen angels or demons?

12:5 **"Male child"** = the Messiah. Revelation 19:15; Psalm 2:9.

12:6 **"Wilderness."** The wilderness is not desolate and foreboding, but symbolic of God's provision for the people of Israel in the Exodus. The idea of nourishment is the key to the symbol. See Deuteronomy 32:11; Exodus 19:4; Deuteronomy 8:3. Elijah was also fed supernaturally in the wilderness (1 Kings 17:6).

"1260 days," that is, the period of persecution. (See the chart on my notes on 11:2 above.) Why is the 3-1/2 period used to characterize this Gospel Age? In addition to its use in Daniel, it is reminiscent of the days of Ahab and Elijah when the rain was withheld by the command of God's prophet (see Revelation 11:6; James 5:17; Luke 4:25; 1 Kings 17:1; 18:1). The faithful Old Testament church was persecuted but not destroyed (1 Kings 19:9-18).

12:7 "Michael and his angels." Described as "one of the chief princes" (Daniel 10:13, 21) and an "archangel" (Jude 9), Michael appears as leader of the heavenly host, the protector of God's people (Daniel 12:1). While Gabriel seems to be an angel of proclamation, Michael is a warlike angel in the struggle against Satan.

"The dragon" (= the Devil and Satan, 12:9) and his angels. These angels are probably fallen angels or demons. See references on 12:4.

12:8 "No longer any place for them in heaven." Satan seems to have had access to God as "the accuser of our brethren". (See Job 1:6-12;

Albrecht Dürer, "St. Michael Fighting the Dragon" (1496), woodcut, 39.4 x 28.3 cm

5. By The Blood of the Lamb (chapters 11-13)

2:1-7; Zechariah 3:1-10.) But since the victory of Christ's full atonement, "Who can bring any charge against God's elect?" (Romans 8:1, 33).

12:9 When Satan was **"thrown down"** from heaven is not stated. This fall was foreseen by Jesus in Luke 10:18. Dispensationalists such as C.C. Ryrie see this as occurring at the middle of the tribulation. More likely, however, this is a heavenly viewpoint symbolic of the victory won by Christ's atonement. (See Colossians 2:15 and John 12:31.) We need not take these "seven mystic figures" in chronological order, but can see them as "repeating patterns."

12:10 **"They have conquered him"** by fearless faith in Christ's atoning blood and their unflinching testimony of Jesus. Though they were killed, they were not made to deny their Lord by Satan's worst – truly they had conquered Satan in their faithful deaths. Here Revelation's theme of faithful witness by the church in times of persecution can be seen with great clarity.

12:13 **"When ... he had been thrown down"** is the beginning of the persecution of God's people who are yet preserved and protected for the 3-1/2 year period (12:6), which I see as the Gospel Age.

12:14 **"Two wings of the great eagle."** This is reminiscent of God's provision of escape for Israel from Pharaoh (Exodus 19:4; Deuteronomy 32:11-12).

12:17 This verse refers to the period of great tribulation during which Satan is successful in decimating the church, that is, **"the rest of her offspring."** (See 13:7.)

Q2. (12:1-17) The vision of the woman and the dragon is heavily symbolic, but comprehensible when you take care to understand. In your own words, what does this vision tell us about the cosmic battle in Jesus' day and in our own? What comfort should we disciples draw from this passage?
http://www.joyfulheart.com/forums/index.php?showtopic=129

Q3. Revelation 12:11 could be considered a theme verse for the book. What does it mean? Who is overcome? In what sense do we have victory if we die in the process? What does the "blood of the Lamb" have to do with this? How does loving our lives prevent spiritual victory today? (See Luke 14:25-27; Matthew 10:37-39.)

http://www.joyfulheart.com/forums/index.php?showtopic=130

The Beast out of the Sea (13:1b-10)

The next vision is of two beasts of satanic origin who bring terrible persecution against the church during the final waning Last Days. See my brief notes on the Antichrist at 11:7 above. The first beast represents the Antichrist, the second the "false prophet."

13:1 "**The beast rising out of the sea**" is a puppet of Satan. He is the Antichrist who is worshipped as in 2 Thessalonians 2:4. The sea represents nations and their governments (Revelation 17:15; Isaiah 17:12). In John's day the Beast from the Sea would have been identified with Rome. This beast symbolizes the persecuting power of Satan embodied in all the nations and governments of the world through all history. The four beasts of Daniel 7

William Blake, "The Great Dragon and the Beast from the Sea" (1805-10), watercolor.

have been combined into this one beast.

"Ten horns and seven heads" shows his relationship to the red dragon of 12:3. See Daniel 7:7; Revelation 17:10. **"A blasphemous name"** may reflect the increasing tendency of Roman emperors to assume titles of deity (see 2 Thessalonians 2:4).

13:3 **"A fatal wound, but the fatal wound had been healed."** We don't know what the Antichrist's "fatal wound" was, but it awes the world and is a noteworthy part of his rise to power (13:12), probably as part of his "counterfeit miracles, signs and wonders" (2 Thessalonians 2:9; Matthew 24:24).

13:5-7 The second 3-1/2 year period (that is, the shorter 3-1/2 day period of Revelation 11:7-11) follows the revelation of the Antichrist = the Beast, in which the beast is **"allowed to make war on the saints and to conquer them."** (See Daniel 7:21-22.)

13:8 **"The book of life of the Lamb that was slain."** (See 3:5; 17:8; 20:12; 21:27.) The names recorded in this book probably correspond with those who have been sealed.

13:10 If one is destined for **"captivity,"** he must be willing to go meekly as a Christian, violent resistance is out of place. But persecution will ultimately be punished with God's **"sword"** of justice (Matthew 26:52). The Christian will need **"endurance"** (one of the key words of Revelation) in the midst of persecution and faith that God will finally avenge injustice. (See 14:12; Matthew 10:22.)

The Beast out of the Earth (13:11-18)

A second beast rises out of the earth and is a servant of the first beast. He is called "the false prophet" (16:13; 19:20; 20:10) and compels people to worship the first beast. He seems to represent organized religion, perhaps reflecting the Roman Imperial priesthood that promoted emperor worship.

13:11 **"Another beast which rose out of the earth."** (See Daniel 7:3, 17.)

"Two horns like a lamb ... spoke like a dragon." He is a parody of Christ, the Lamb of God. The first beast represents civil power, satanically inspired; the second beast represents religious power employed to support civil power.

13:14 **"Deceives"** by signs and miracles. (See 2 Thessalonians 2:9-10; Matthew 24:24.)

13:16 The Mark of the Beast is in contrast to the sealing of God's servants (7:3-4). It will come down to a person either bearing the mark of the beast or the seal of God. There is no middle ground. "The Lord knows those who are his" (2 Timothy 2:19). Religious tattooing was widespread in the ancient world (Mounce).

13:17 "Buy or sell." The mark allows economic freedom. Only those who would rather die than compromise their faith will resist the mark of Antichrist. But there has been a lot of foolishness taught about the Mark of the Beast. I can remember when the USB codes on packages were suspect!

Q4. (13:1-18, optional) The two beasts belong to the period of the ascendancy of the Antichrist at the very end of the Last Days. Together with 2 Thessalonians 2:1-12, summarize what have you learned about the Antichrist and the False Prophet.
http://www.joyfulheart.com/forums/index.php?showtopic=131

William Blake, "The Number of the Beast is 666" (1805-10), watercolor

13:18 "The number of the beast ... is 666." Neither Hebrew or Greek used a system of numbers like the Arabic numerals we use today. In ancient times the letters of the alphabet served as numbers, a practice called gematria. The first nine letters stood for 1 through 9, the next 9 letters for 10 through 90, etc. Thus every name yielded a number. Graffiti from Pompeii reads, for example, "I love her whose number is 545." The *Sibylline Oracles* 1:325 converts "Jesus" in Greek (ΙΗΣΟΥΣ) into the number 888 (Ι = 10, Η = 8, Σ = 200, Ο = 70, γ = 400, Σ = 200).

There have been numerous ancient and modern theories, all unconvincing. Almost anything can be done with numbers by clever manipulation and a great deal of foolishness has attended the puzzle of 666. A few examples:

1. The numerical total of the Greek title of **Emperor Nero** is 666 when transliterated into the Hebrew alphabet and the spelling altered slightly.
2. The **Latin title of the pope**, *Vicarivs fillii dei* (Vicar of the Son of God) = 666 if only the values of the letters of the title which represent Roman numerals are totaled.
3. Taking A=6, B= 6+6, C= 6+ 6+ 6, etc., the words **"Kissinger"** and **"Computer"** add up to 666.
4. If A = 100, B=101, C=102, etc., **"Hitler"** totals 666.

Some have seen the number as symbolic of the number which falls short of perfection in each of its digits. "This evil trinity apes the Holy Trinity 777, but always falls short and fails" (Torrance). This seems to be part of John's vision which is "sealed up" until those days when the Church needs to recognize the revealed Antichrist.

Chapters 11, 12, and 13 offer different visions and symbolic figures, all of which teach a similar lesson: The faithful, witnessing Church will antagonize enemies in the world, who are, in fact, dupes of Satan and part of a larger cosmic spiritual warfare between Satan and God. Though the Church will have considerable time to bear witness, a time will come when Satan's ascendancy is so great that the Church is seemingly crushed. But even then, Satan does not triumph, because:

> "But they have conquered him by the blood of the Lamb
> and by the word of their testimony,
> for they did not cling to life even in the face of death." (Revelation 12:11, NRSV)

Prayer

Lord, embolden us as we read Revelation so that we might be willing to bear testimony to you "in season and out of season." Keep us from being intimidated by those who are angered at any mention of God and of Jesus. Help us to avoid being overly obnoxious in our testimony, but not so subtle that our testimony is watered down to the point of being impotent. Give us wisdom. Help us as we prepare for the terrible times that face your Church in the Last Days. In Jesus' name, we pray. Amen.

6. Alas, Babylon! (chapters 14-18)

As history races to its final conclusion we see a great homecoming and rejoicing in heaven and massive wailing and judgment on earth.

1. The Lamb and the 144,000 in heaven
2. Three angels announcing grace, doom, and warning
3. The harvest of the righteous on the earth
4. The harvest of the wicked on the earth
5. The Seven Bowls of God's wrath upon the earth
6. A vision of Babylon as a prostitute
7. The fall of Babylon

William Blake, "The Whore of Babylon" (1809), pen and watercolor over pencil, 266 x 233 mm, British Museum, London.

What seemed so exciting and glorious about a prosperous city and its world trade now turns to doom as the city falls and burns. The glitter of the world is tarnished as the true glory is revealed. Let's examine these visions.

The Lamb and the 144,000 (14:1-5)

14:1 "144,000" are sealed in their foreheads, in contrast to the followers and worshippers of the beast. In 7:3-4 they seemed to be on the earth. Now they are before the throne of God in heaven. See my notes on 7:3 in Lesson 4 concerning the identity of the 144,000 as the whole Church.

14:3-5 A number of characteristics of these 144,000 are given:

7. The Millennium (chapters 19-20)

1. **"Redeemed from the earth"** (5:9-10).
2. **"Chaste,"** Greek "virgins." This probably refers to either those who refrained from adultery or sexual immorality (see the temptations in the churches of Pergamum and Thyatira, chapter 2), or those who have kept themselves pure from all defiling relationships with the pagan world system. (Compare 2 Kings 19:21; Jeremiah 18:13; 2 Corinthians 11:2; Revelation 17:2; 21:9.) However, this symbol differs from the usual depiction of Israel as a female virgin, betrothed or married to Yahweh.
3. **"Follow the Lamb wherever he goes"** (Mark 8:34; John 10:27).
4. **"First fruits."** The word can be used as the beginning of the harvest with more to follow (1 Corinthians 15:20, 23), but also as that portion of the harvest which is wholly dedicated and given as an offering to God (James 1:18; Jeremiah 2:3).
5. **"No lie."** (See 22:15; 21:27; Zephaniah 3:13.) Truthfulness is characteristic of the Messiah's followers.
6. **"Spotless,"** ethically blameless (Ephesians 1:4; 5:27; Colossians 1:22). We are made spotless before God only by washing our robes in the atoning blood of the Lamb (7:14). "This cup is the new covenant in my blood, which is poured out for many for the forgiveness of sins" (Matthew 26:28).

In short, I believe these 144,000 are not a select group, but an ideal representation all Christians who are followers of the Lord.

Q1. (14:3-5) In what ways do the 144,000 provide an ideal for all Christians to emulate?
http://www.joyfulheart.com/forums/index.php?showtopic=132

The Three Angels (14:6-13)

14:6 "An angel flying in midheaven." Three angels present three interrelated and progressive proclamations:

1. Summons to worship God,
2. Prediction of the downfall of the great capital city of paganism, and
3. A vivid portrayal of those who worship the beast.

14:8 "Babylon the great." As the ancient Mesopotamian city had become the political and religious capital of a world empire, noted for its luxury and moral corruption, so Rome was a contemporary Babylon, the great enemy of God's people in New Testament times. More on this in Chapter 18. In Jewish and Christian circles, "Babylon" was becoming a symbolic title for Rome, with examples in 1 Peter 5:13 and other apocalyptic literature of the time (J.N.D. Kelly, *Epistles of Peter and of Jude* [Harper's NT Commentaries; Harper, 1969], p. 218.)

14:10 "The wine of God's wrath," a common Old Testament metaphor of divine punishment (Job 21:20; Psalm 75:8; Isaiah 51:17; Jeremiah 25:15-28).

"Tormented with fire and sulfur," recalls the judgments on Sodom and Gomorrah (Genesis 19:24; Luke 17:29-30; Revelation 19:20; 20:10; 21:8).

14:11 "Torment ... for ever and ever ... no rest." Eternal punishment is the antithesis of eternal life and rest. As one is conscious, so is the other. This is not unloving, but the logical requirement of justice for those who have rebelled against their Maker and spurned his mercy. It is difficult for moderns to understand such awesome justice. We are more merciful than that, we say. But Jesus himself – the Master of mercy, the very One from whom we learned to be merciful – used very similar language to describe hell. (See Matthew 25:41, 46; 26:24; Mark 9:43-49; Luke 16:19-31; 2 Thessalonians 1:5-10.)

Q2. (14:10-11) Why is everlasting punishment so difficult for us Christians to accept? In what ways might eternal punishment be considered just punishment?
http://www.joyfulheart.com/forums/index.php?showtopic=133

14:13 "Blessed are the dead who die in the Lord henceforth." An encouragement to those who are called upon to face martyrdom for their endurance (14:12).

The Harvest of the Earth (14:14-20)

14:14 "One like a son of man." This phrase is quoted from Daniel 7:13, and no doubt refers to the Messiah, who called himself "the Son of Man."

14:15 "Put in your sickle and reap for the harvest of the earth is fully ripe." (See Joel 3:13.) This harvest may include both the righteous (Matthew 9:37-38; Mark 4:29; John 4:35-38) and the unrighteous (Matthew 13:30, 40-42; also Jeremiah 51:33; Hosea 6:11). This is a general picture of coming judgment.

14:19 "The winepress of the wrath of God." This is surely not a mixed harvest, but stressed the violent carnage of the judgment of the Messiah at his coming (Revelation 19:11-21; Joel 3:13-14; Isaiah 63:3; Lamentations 1:15). This passage has inspired several Christian hymns, among which are:

- **"The Battle Hymn of the Republic,"** by Julia Ward Howe:

    "Mine eyes have seen the glory of the coming of the Lord;
    He is trampling out the vintage where the grapes of wrath are stored;
    He hath loosed the fateful lightning of His terrible swift sword;
    His truth is marching on.

    "He has sounded for the trumpet that shall never sound retreat;
    He is sifting out the hearts of men before His judgment seat...."

- **"Come, Ye Thankful People Come"** by Henry Alford, which we commonly sing at Thanksgiving in America, includes the theme of the harvesting of the wheat and the tares.

Seven Angels with Seven Plagues (15:1-8)

15:1 "Seven plagues which are the last." The bowl plagues are total, in contrast to the seals (1/4 destroyed; chapters 6 to 8) and the trumpets (1/3 destroyed; chapters 8 to 9). The opportunity for repentance is gone. These have rejected the Lamb and worshipped the beast, now hardened in their impenitence. Instead of repentance or awe (11:13), their response is to curse God (16:9, 11, 21). Notice the parallels with the plagues and deliverance of Exodus.

15:2 "Those who had conquered the beast." (See 12:11; 13:15.) They conquered by not denying their Christ upon pain of death. What more could Satan do to them? See Matthew 10:28-33.

15:3 "The song of Moses ... and the song of the Lamb." The saints on the shore of the sea of glass sing a song celebrating God's victory, just as Moses and the people of Israel did on the shores of the Red Sea (Exodus 15:1-18). This is not two but one song celebrating God's righteous and redemptive work beginning with Moses and culminating in the Lamb.

I am impressed with all the praise we are shown in heaven. Much of it sounds like praise choruses: a personal, direct worship of God for his righteousness and worthiness.

Q3. (15:3-4) We see singing and praise in heaven before the throne a number of times in Revelation (4:8, 11; 5:9-10, 12-13; 7:12; 11:17-18; 15:3-4; 19:1-3). What do you learn about appropriate worship from studying these songs? Do you recognize any contemporary songs that seem similar to these?

http://www.joyfulheart.com/forums/index.php?showtopic=134

15:5 "The tent of testimony" (Exodus 38:21; Numbers 1:50) contained the two tables of testimony, the Ten Commandments, God's covenant with Israel. This is another reference to the typology of the Exodus deliverance.

15:7 "Seven golden bowls." Greek *phialē*, like our word "vial". But this is not like our "vial", but a wide shallow bowl or cup, usually without a stand or foot.

15:8 "The temple was filled with smoke." (See Exodus 19:18; 40:34; 1 Kings 8:10-11; Isaiah 6:4.)

The Seven Bowls of God's Wrath (16:1-21)

16:2 "Foul and evil sores." "Sore, abscess, ulcer" (BDAG 317-318). See the sixth Egyptian plague (Exodus 9:9-11). Only the beast's followers suffer; God's people are protected.

16:3 "Sea ... became like the blood of a dead man," that is, coagulated and rotting. See the first Egyptian plague (Exodus 7:20-21) and the second trumpet (8:8-9).

16:4 "Rivers and fountains became blood." Similar to the third trumpet (8:10-11) but now afflicts all the fresh water.

16:6 There is a grim appropriateness in this plague. Those who shed Christian blood must now drink blood.

16:7 "The altar," here personified, reminds us of the cry of the martyrs for justice (6:9; 8:3-5). The opportunity for mercy is past.

16:8 "Scorch men with fire." The sun once darkened (8:12) now brings the judgment of fire (Deuteronomy 28:22; 1 Corinthians 3:13; 2 Peter 3:7, 10). Contrast the protection of the saints in 7:16.

16:10 "The throne of the beast ... its kingdom was in darkness." This supernatural darkness is directed against the Antichrist's godless, worldly domain. There is torment and his followers are confused but impenitent. See the ninth Egyptian plague (Exodus 10:21-23).

16:12 "The great river Euphrates ... dried up to prepare the way for the kings from the East." God sets the stage for the final conflict in which the world's armies are slain. (See Exodus 14:21; Joshua 3:14-17.)

16:13 "The false prophet" is "the beast from the earth" (13:11-18), the religious power supporting the civil power of the Antichrist. (See Revelation 13:14; 19:20; 20:10.)

16:14 "The kings of the whole world ... assembled for battle." The ten kings first make war on Babylon and destroy it (17:16-18). Then they gather for battle against the Lamb. The result of the battle is given in 19:11-21. Demonically inspired to battle, the kings and their armies are destroyed by the conquering Messiah, and the beast and false prophet are thrown into the lake of fire. These kings may include Gog, ruler of Magog (Ezekiel 38-39), also referred to in Revelation 20:7-8. (See also Zechariah 14:1-5 and Joel 3:2.)

16:15 "Like a thief." (See 1 Thessalonians 5:2; Matthew 24:42-44; 2 Peter 3:10; Revelation 3:3.) This may be an indication that Christians are still present on the earth.

16:16 "Armageddon," Hebrew for "the hill of Megiddo," probably the tell mound of the ancient city of Megiddo about 70 feet high, overlooking the Valley of Jezreel, the site of many great Old Testament battles.

16:18 "A great earthquake" destroys Babylon and all the cities of the nations. Babylon has first been burned by the ten

The Tell or Mountain of Megiddo (Armageddon) rising above the Jezreel Valley where the final battle will be fought.

kings (17:16-18), and now is destroyed by earthquake with the kings' cities. It seems that the sixth and seventh bowls are detailed in chapters 17-19.

16:21 "Hailstones." (See Joshua 10:11; Ezekiel 38:22; Revelation 8:7; 11:19.)

The Woman on the Beast (17:1-18)

17:1 "The great harlot." Wilcox (pp. 156-160) notes the various characteristics of the Whore of Babylon:

1. **Influential.** She is enthroned over all the nations (17:1-2, 15), and has the inhabitants of the earth and their kings in her power. All are taken in by her wiles.
2. **Evil.** The power that supports her is the satanic Antichrist (17:3).
3. **Attractive** (17:4). The simple soul is likely to be dazzled by the Beauty before he notices the Beast. Even John finds himself marveling (17:6b).
4. **Repulsive.** What has made her drunk is her apparent victory over those who witness to the Christian truth she hates (17:6a), and for that she will be shunned by all who hold truth dear.

Who is this Whore of Babylon? She is Rome (17:9, 18), but she is more than that. She represents, human civilization – the world with all its wealth, power, and luxury – organized in opposition to God (1 John 2:15-17). Jesus was offered "Babylon" and rejected its temptations in Matthew 4:89. The Whore of Babylon has as her opposite the pure Bride of Christ (19:7-9) and the Holy City of God, New Jerusalem (chapters 21-22).

1. **Harlotry** is a common Old Testament symbol for religious apostasy (Isaiah 1:21; 23:16-17; Ezekiel 16:15-18; Nahum 3:4), which allures, tempts, seduces, and draws people away from God.
2. Babylon is a **worldly city**. In Revelation 18:11-15, Babylon is seen as a great commercial metropolis. This indicates the world as a center of industry, commerce, art, culture – the embodiment of "the lust of the flesh, the lust of the eyes, and the pride of life" (1 John 2:16; see Luke 8:14).
3. Babylon in John's day was **embodied in Rome**, "the city on the seven hills" (17:9). Yet, though its form changes from one period of history to another, its essence remains. Babylon is the world as the center of antichristian seduction at any time in history (Hendriksen). The call, "Come out of her, my people, lest you take part in her sins, lest you share in her plagues," is as imperative for us today as it was for the

rich, adulterous, idolatrous Christians of the churches of Asia (chapters 2-3; see 2 Corinthians 6:16-18). "Be zealous and repent. Behold I stand at the door" (Revelation 3:19-20).

4. The Whore's **golden cup** (17:4) which she offers contains nothing but abominations to lead people away from God and defile them.

17:2 "many waters" = "peoples, multitudes, nations, and tongues" (17:15).

17:3 "Scarlet beast" = the beast from the sea (13:1), the Antichrist, now with the blood-red color of its master, the red dragon.

17:8 "The beast ... was, and is not, and is to ascend from the bottomless pit and go into perdition." This is a parody of the Lamb (1:4, 8; 4:8). The beast's present absence is probably due to the mortal wound on one of his heads (13:3, 12, 14), from which he recovers. The Battle of Armageddon is his last rise and banishment to perdition (that is, destruction), the lake of fire (19:19-21).

17:11 "It is an eighth, but it belongs to the seven." The beast's own reign as Antichrist is separate, but similar to and a culmination of the reign of the seven kings/kingdoms (see Daniel, chapters 2 and 7, Ladd 229-230; Hendriksen, 204-205; Alford 4:710-711).

17:12 "Ten horns ... are ten kings." These are colleagues and supporters of the Antichrist for a short time, one hour. They gather for the Battle of Armageddon where they are defeated (17:14; 19:11-21).

17:16 The ten kings and the Antichrist now attack the city which has world dominion and destroy it. Babylon once held ascendancy, Rome in John's day. Which is it today? Washington? London? Paris? Is America the center of present-day Babylon? (17:18).

The Fall of Babylon (18:1-24)

Chapter 18 is a series of dirges raised over the fallen city of Babylon. The imagery is drawn from a number of Old Testament themes and passages.

18:2 Isaiah 13:21-22; 21:9; Revelation 14:8.

18:4 Isaiah 52:11; Jeremiah 51:45; 2 Corinthians 6:17.

Q4. (18:4) We Christians are instructed to be "in the world" but not "of the world" (John 17:15-19). One interpretation has been to be hermits, ascetics, to distance ourselves from the political process, and to adopt stringent dress and behavior codes. Another interpretation is to be "salt and light" (Matthew 5:13-16) in the world so that we might bring about cleansing and change through God's spirit. Where do you think the balance lies? How and when should we fulfill the command, "Come out of her, my people, so that you will not share in her sins...."?
http://www.joyfulheart.com/forums/index.php?showtopic=135

18:7 Isaiah 47:7-8.

18:9-19 Compare Ezekiel 27. The kings of the earth, whose political destinies were tied with Babylon's, mourn (18:9-10). Then the merchants who will be ruined by a loss of their lucrative markets mourn (18:11-17a). Finally the shipping industry which supplied her transportation network mourns at this loss of trade (18:17b-19).

18:21-24 This passage recalls the prophetic act of Jeremiah the prophet concerning literal Babylon (Jeremiah 51:59-64). Babylon sinks to rise no more. Now violence reigns, followed by stillness (see Jeremiah 25:10).

18:24 The blood of prophets and of saints is finally avenged.

Prayer

Father, show us how to live fully in your Kingdom while we dwell in the midst of this corrupt and luxurious world. Show us how to love rather than to remain aloof. Show us how to be Jesus' servants in this very needy world. In Jesus' name, we pray. Amen.

7. The Millennium (chapters 19-20)

Now John's vision begins to reach its consummation with the victory of Christ over his enemies. As you study these two chapters, look for how God might speak to you through them.

Praise from the Heavenly Multitude (19:1-10)

19:1-5 The multitude's joy springs from justice, not mere gloating over the punishment of the enemy for the sake of spite.

19:6 "A great multitude" comprises all God's servants (19:5), the completed, raptured church. These seem to be the same ones seen in the vision of Revelation 7:9-17 in white robes who "have come out of the great tribulation."

Flemish painter Hieronymus Bosch (c1450-1516) shows great imagination in his triptych altarpiece "The Last Judgment" (c1510-15), center panel, Academy, Vienna.

19:7 "The marriage of the Lamb has come." The metaphor of marriage as expressing the relationship between God and his people has its roots in the Old Testament prophets (Ezekiel 16:8; Isaiah 50:1; 54:1-8; 62:5; Hosea 2:14-23) and is carried through the New Testament (Matthew 9:15; John 3:29; 2 Corinthians 11:2; Ephesians 5:32; Revelation 21:2, 9; 22:17). Notice these elements in a Jewish marriage:

1. **Betrothal**. More binding than our "engagement." The groom and bride are legally husband and wife and, as such, are under obligations of faithfulness.
2. An **interval** separates the betrothal from the actual wedding ceremony.
3. The groom and his company proceeds to the bride's house to receive her.
4. The bride and groom and procession **go to the groom's house or his parents' house** for the completion of the marriage and the **marriage feast**. See the hymn "The Church's One Foundation", verse 1:

   "... From heav'n he came and sought her to be his holy bride,
   With his own blood he bought her, and for her life he died."
   – Samuel J. Stone, 1866

19:8 **"The fine linen is the righteous deeds of the saints."** Contrast the bride's pure attire with the harlot's gaudy purple and scarlet (17:4). The phrase "was given her" reveals that the robes were given to the saints, not provided by them. The white robes of 7:9, 14 were a result of washing "in the blood of the Lamb." But, seeing that righteousness is entirely by grace, not works, we are "created in Christ Jesus for good works" (Ephesians 2:8-10), the fruit of the Spirit-filled life.

19:9 **"The marriage supper of the Lamb"** is the fulfillment of the promises of Luke 12:37; 13:28; 14:15-24; 22:30; Matthew 8:11; 26:29.

Q1. (19:7-9) These verses draw together two themes from Scripture – (1) God's people as his betrothed Bride and (2) the feast of all God's people in heaven. When you meditate on these themes, how are you both admonished and encouraged?
http://www.joyfulheart.com/forums/index.php?showtopic=136

19:10 **"The testimony of Jesus is the spirit of prophecy"** (John 5:39; Luke 24:27; 1 Corinthians 12:3). This oft-quoted sentence is a bit ambiguous in Greek and its exact meaning is disputed by scholars. The clause "of Jesus" could mean the "testimony which Jesus gives or inspires" (subjective genitive) or could refer to "testimony concerning Jesus" (objective genitive). Likewise, the second clause "the spirit of prophecy" could mean "Spirit-inspired prophecy" (subjective genitive) or perhaps "the principle that dominates prophecy" (objective genitive). However, in light of the fact that "the Spirit of prophecy" was a traditional Jewish name for the Spirit of God, it is likely that this phrase means, "The testimony borne by Jesus is the concern

The Rider on the White Horse (19:11-21)

19:11 "White horse." White is a symbol of victory. Note in 6:2 the white horse and rider wearing a crown, "Conquering and to conquer." There the rider didn't seem to represent the Messiah. Here it surely does.

"Faithful and True" (Revelation 1:5; 3:14; 21:5; 22:6).

"In righteousness he judges and makes war." (2 Thessalonians 1:7-10; 2:8; Psalm 96:13; Acts 17:31; Hebrews 9:27-28). The Jews expected a military, conquering Messiah. His second advent will fulfill those prophecies they had pointed to, such as Psalm 2:6-10 and Zechariah 14.

19:12 "Eyes like a flame of fire" (Revelation 1:14; 2:18).

"Many crowns." He has many diadems or crowns since he is "King of kings" (19:16), in contrast to Satan's usurpation of power (12:3; 13:1). The hymn "Crown Him With Many Crowns" takes its title from this verse.

19:13 "A robe dipped in blood." Not his own blood, but as Isaiah 63:1-6, the blood of the slain foes (19:15b).

19:15 References are to Isaiah 11:4, 63:3; Psalm 2:9; 2 Thessalonians 2:8. (See also Revelation 2:27; 14:19-20.)

19:16 His victory over the kings of the earth (verse 19) demonstrates his title: **"King of kings and Lord of lords"** (Ezra 7:12; Ezekiel 26:7; Daniel 2:37; Philippians 2:9-11; Revelation 17:14). This title is applied both to the God the Father and to the Son (1 Timothy 6:15).

Q2. (19:16) What are the implications of Christ's title: "King of kings and Lord of lords" for your life? For the everyday world that surrounds you?
http://www.joyfulheart.com/forums/index.php?showtopic=137

19:17 "The great supper of God." This gruesome scene is viewed in Ezekiel 39:17-20 where it is called a "sacrificial feast." What a contrast to the "marriage supper of the

Lamb" (verse 9)! This vision emphasizes the greatness and universality of the coming slaughter.

19:18 "The beast and the kings ... gathered to make war." This is the Battle of Armageddon (16:16). See my notes and references at 16:14.

19:20 "The beast and the false prophet" are, respectively, the "beast from the sea" (13:1-8) – the Antichrist – and "the beast from the earth" (13:11-18), that is, religious power in support of the civil power of the Antichrist.

"The lake of fire" later provides the final end of the devil (20:10) and those who were not followers of the Lamb (20:14-15; 21:8; Matthew 5:22; 25:41).

The Thousand Years (20:1-15)

Chapter 20 is one of the most debated chapters in Revelation. The issue is the place of the "millennium" (which means "1,000 years") in the scheme of End Times events. There are four main schools of thought.[1] Be sure to print out the Chronologies of the Millennium and Christ's Return chart from Appendix 2 so you can visualize these four views.

1. **Historic pre-millennialism** teaches that the order of events is: tribulation, rapture, millennium, new heavens and earth.
2. **Dispensationalism pre-millennialism** teaches this order: "secret rapture" of the believers, tribulation, Christ's return, millennium, new heavens and new earth.
3. **Amillennialism** is really a misnomer, for amillennialists believe that the millennium (seen as Christ's heavenly rule) coincides with the Gospel age and tribulation. Christ's return and rapture are followed immediately by the new heavens and new earth.
4. **Post-millennialism** sees the conflict between good and evil on earth as gradually giving way to the fullness of the kingdom and victory of the church which is the millennium, followed by Christ's coming in judgment and the new heavens and new earth.

---

[1] These are discussed in detail by major exponents of each view in the excellent book *The Meaning of the Millennium: Four Views*, edited by Robert G. Clouse (InterVarsity Press, 1977). If you're trying to get a handle on this subject, I strongly recommend for you to study this book to get a fairly-presented case for, and implications of, each view. Of these four views, only the second teaches the pre-tribulation rapture.

7. The Millennium (chapters 19-20)

Chronologies of the Millennium and Christ's Return
Theories of the Order of Events

Great Tribulation — The "7 year" period marking the rise of the Antichrist, increase of evil, persecution of Christians (Matthew 24:21, 29; 2 Thessalonians 2:1-12; Revelation 7:14;), just prior to Christ's return in glory (Matthew 24:30-31; Acts 1:11). One's theory of the time of the rapture is described as pre-trib, mid-trib, or post-trib.

Rapture — (from Latin *raptus*, "snatch away"), the catching up of Christians to meet Christ in the End Time (Matthew 24:29-31; 1 Corinthians 15:51-52; 1 Thessalonians 4:13-18; 2 Thessalonians 2:1).

Millennium — "1,000 year" period of Christ's earthly reign, during which time Satan is bound (Revelation 20:1-6). One's theory of the timing of Christ's return is described as pre-millennial or post-millennial (before or after the millennium). Amillennialists believe the millennium is not a literal period time, but coincides with the Church Age.

Church Age — The period of time the Church has to declare the Gospel before Christ's return (Matthew 24:14; Luke 21:24; Romans 11:25)

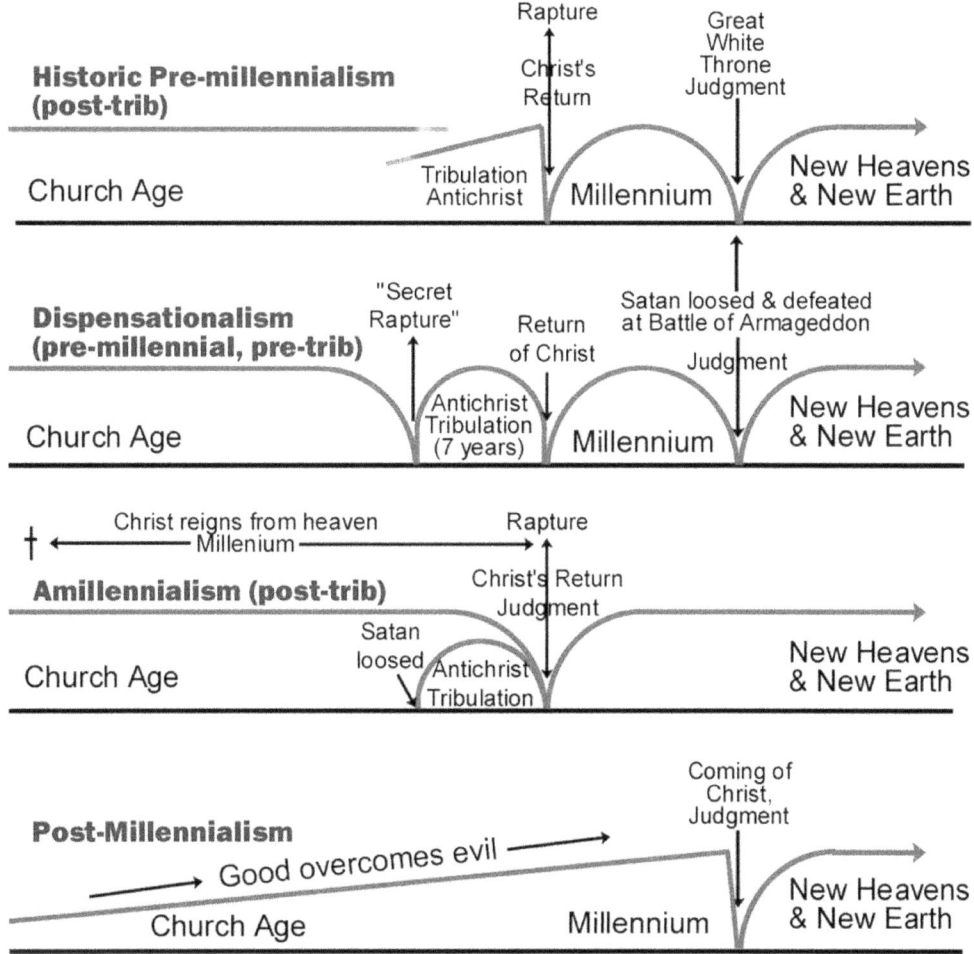

Copyright © 2011, Ralph F. Wilson pastor@joyfulheart.com *Revelation: Discipleship Lessons* www.jesuswalk.com/revelation

Few adherents of post-millennialism remain because of disillusionment following the World Wars of the twentieth century. Dispensationalism's pre-tribulation rapture is the newest of the four theories.

The Dispensationalist chronology is said to have first been prophesied by a woman in the Irvingite Movement in mid-nineteenth century England and spread to America through the writing and lectures of J.N. Darby (Plymouth Brethren), and later, C.I. Scofield, and the Bible College movement.[2] Of the various theories, I see the most Scriptural support for Historic Pre-Millennialism (post- or mid-trib variety).

20:1 "Key of the bottomless pit." See my notes on 9:2.

20:2 "He seized the dragon ... and bound him for a thousand years" (2 Peter 2:4; Jude 6). Amillennialists see this section as a recapitulation of the history of the church from another viewpoint. That the binding of Satan is figurative for the restraint of Satan's power suggested in Matthew 12:29; Luke 10:18; Revelation 12:9; and 2 Thessalonians 2:7. They take the thousand years as figurative for the period from Christ's ascension to the appearance of the Antichrist. They see the release of Satan (20:3, 7) as equivalent to the revelation of the Antichrist. They identify the Battle of Armageddon (16:16; 17:13-14; 19:11-21) with the Battle of Gog and Magog (20:8-9).

The flaw with this view, in my opinion, is the necessity of spiritualizing the **"first resurrection"** (19:4-6). The judgment of Babylon (chapters 17-18) must precede the reign of the martyrs (19:4) who were seen previously (6:9-11) as awaiting vengeance and the completion of their number. In addition, a comparison of 19:20 and 20:10 seems to prohibit any idea of recapitulation here.

20:4 "Thrones ... those to whom judgment was committed" (1 Corinthians 6:2; 2 Timothy 2:12; Daniel 7:9; Matthew 19:28; Daniel 7:22). This may be a reference to the whole church's reign with Christ.

"Those who had been beheaded." I believe all Christians will share in the reign, but the spotlight is on the now-vindicated martyrs (see 6:9-11).

"Come to life," a reference to the resurrection of believers (1 Thessalonians 4:14-17; 1 Corinthians 15:51-52). A similar way of speaking of resurrection is found in 11:11 where the two witnesses (= the church, see notes on 11:1) come alive again.

---

[2] A critique of the Dispensationalist view is detailed in *The Incredible Cover-Up: Exposing the Origins of Rapture Theories*, by Dave MacPherson (Omega Publications, 1983).

7. The Millennium (chapters 19-20)

"A thousand years." This may be literal, but is probably figurative of a long time. The number "thousand" was often used generically as a large number, something like how we use "a million" (Psalm 50:10 and 2 Peter 3:8).

"The rest of the dead" probably refers to the unbelievers. This time separation between the resurrection of the just and the unjust was not made explicit in earlier Scriptures (Daniel 12:2; John 5:28-29; Acts 24:15). These unbelievers are raised at the end of the millennium to be judged (20:11-13).

You may wonder: **Over whom** do the martyrs and saints rule? This question is not answered in the text. The most likely assumption from the text is that the survivors of the tribulation are the subjects. Whether saved or unsaved we are not told. However, the children of these original millennialists may not follow the religion of their parents. A choice will be theirs. Even without Satan's active deception (20:3), the unregenerate heart is rebellious. Many will follow Satan when he is again loosed (20:7).

Some Dispensationalists see this as a time when the promises to the literal Jews (the 144,000 of the tribulation, as they see it) are now literally fulfilled, such as the building of Ezekiel's temple (Ezekiel 40-48). However, it is very difficult to decide which Old Testament prophecies speak of the millennium (if any) and which speak of the new heavens and the new earth. We know from the Epistle to the Hebrews that the Jewish sacrificial system is obsolete after Christ's complete sacrifice (Hebrews 8:13; 9:12; 10:18), nor do we see any indication that a literal temple or tabernacle will be rebuilt under Messiah's reign (Hebrews 8:1-2; 9:11).

Why is there a millennium prior to the new heavens and new earth? We are not told. However, it may be:

1. A reward for the martyrs to reign over it with Christ (Mounce), and
2. A demonstration of the corruption of the human heart despite the best environment, that is, a vindication of God's righteous judgment which cannot be put off by the excuse: "It isn't fair."

20:8 The final battle between the nations will involve Gog and Magog against the "camp of the saints" at Jerusalem (Ezekiel 38-39). There are a number of similarities with the battle of Armageddon.

20:10 "Tormented day and night forever." This not annihilation, as some teach, but eternal, conscious torment in the lake of fire. See my notes on 14:10-11.

20:11 "A great white throne." See Revelation 4 and 5. All mankind is summoned before God. This is the time of the second resurrection, presumably of the unjust. It may also be the time of judgment of Christians, described also as "the judgment seat of God" (Romans 14:10-12) and "the judgment seat of Christ" (2 Corinthians 5:10). However, Christians are not in danger of damnation like the unbelievers (John 5:24; 1 Corinthians 3:12-15), but are vindicated in the process and their names are found in the Lamb's book of life (20:12).

20:12 "Books were opened" (Daniel 7:10). This is a record of the deeds of each person. A reading will show the pure justice of God's verdict.

"The book of life." A list of those "recorded for life in Jerusalem" (Isaiah 4:3; Daniel 12:1). Alford (4:735) writes: "Those books and the book of life bore independent witness to the fact of men being or not being among the saved – the one by inference from the works recorded, the other by inscription or non-inscription of the name in the list."

Q3. (20:11-12) Why is this awesome scene of judgment so frightening? Why do people seem to resist the idea of a final judgment?
http://www.joyfulheart.com/forums/index.php?showtopic=138

Q4. (20:12-15) Here is a serious question for each of us – not one we should respond to with pat answers. What assurance do you have that your name is written in the Book of Life?
http://www.joyfulheart.com/forums/index.php?showtopic=139

If you need to know how to receive Christ as your Savior, please consider the simple Four Spiritual Laws (www.jesuswho.org/english/four.htm). Also, feel free to contact me. Perhaps I can help guide you towards Christ.

20:14 "Death and Hades were thrown into the lake of fire." This is a symbolic way of saying: "Death shall be no more (21:4).

20:15 "Not found written in the book." A person is either a follower of Christ or not, there is no middle ground. A great many follow the broad road (Matthew 7:13), are deceived by the Whore of Babylon (Revelation 17-18) and the glitter of riches (1

7. The Millennium (chapters 19-20)

John 2:15-17; Matthew 13:22), and do not seek life from Jesus. Their displacement of Christ's lordship in favor of money (Matthew 6:24) is rebellion. The result of that rejection is the lake of fire.

The chapters we have just studied are controversial. But let's not get hung up on the things we can't be sure of – especially the exact chronology of the rapture and the millennium. What we can be sure of are the certainty of Christ's victory over the world and Satan, of judgment, of reward and of punishment. These things are clear – and awesome.

Prayer

Lord, these are fearful chapters. Our world would tell us that judgment will never come, that we can flaunt God's laws and get away with it. But as I read of this terrible judgment, I am aware of my own sins. I need your forgiveness, Lord, and believe that you have forgiven me through your grace. Thank you for writing my name in the Lamb's Book of Life. I am not worthy, but you have made me worthy. In Jesus' name, I thank you. Amen.

8. We Shall See His Face (chapters 21-22)

Revelation's scenes of hardship, persecution, and judgment now fade to the background. The final chapters bring into sharp focus the joy of God's people in God's presence. Much here is symbolic language, not literal, so don't expect all the figures to match exactly. John is expressing heavenly, spiritual realities in human language that has literally no words to describe them. In part, he is describing God's incredible love for his church, pictured here as the City of God. Relax and enjoy this vision's beauty, clarity, and promise for you in the words that tumble from John's pen.

William Blake, "The River of Life" (1805), pen and watercolor, 305 x 336 mm, London, Tate Gallery, National Gallery of British Art

The New Jerusalem (21:1-27)

21:1 "A new heaven and a new earth" (20:11; 21:5; Isaiah 65:17; 66:22; Romans 8:19-23; 2 Peter 3:13). The conclusion of the last book in the Bible reveals the completion of those elements begun in Genesis, the book of beginnings. See some of the comparisons:

8. We Shall See His Face (chapters 21-22)

Genesis	Revelation
1:1 God created the heavens and the earth	21:1 God creates a new heaven and a new earth
1:14-19 God creates the sun and moon.	21:23 City has no need of sun or moon, glory of God, Lamb, its light.
3:23 Paradise is lost	2:7; 22:2-3 Paradise is restored
3:8 Man flees and hides from God	21:3; 22:4 Full communion with God is restored
3:22 Tree of life denied Adam	2:7; 22:14 Tree of life offered man
3:1-7 Satan deceives man	20:10 Satan is destroyed

21:1 "Had passed away." The method is purging by fire. (See 2 Peter 3:10-13.)

"The sea was no more." The sea was associated with ideas of evil and rebellion (13:1; 17:1, 15; Isaiah 57:20).

21:2 "The holy city, new Jerusalem" = the Bride, the wife of the Lamb (21:9-10; 3:12; Hebrews 12:22-24). Jerusalem is more than an actual physical city now, but a symbol of the Church in its perfected and eternal state. "The consummation of the Christian hope is supremely social ... life in the redeemed community of heaven" (Hunter). A number of times in the Bible the people of God are represented as a city. Moreover, Jerusalem or Zion becomes a symbol for God's people (Isaiah 26:1; 40:1, 9; Psalm 48; Galatians 4:26; Revelation 12:22-23). Augustine's famous work on the church is entitled *The City of God*. Jerusalem – always the center of Old Testament prophecy – now finds fulfillment.

21:3 "Behold, the dwelling of God is with men." As with many features of these two chapters, what is true of the Christian today in part will be made complete in that day. Now we have an "earnest" or "down payment" of the Spirit, "the guarantee of our inheritance until we acquire possession of it" (Ephesians 1:13-14. See also John 14:23; Ezekiel 37:27; 2 Corinthians 1:22; 5:5; 6:16).

Q1. (21:3-5) What is the significance of the fact that in heaven "God himself will be with them"? Why can the promises in 21:4 only be fulfilled in heaven? Which of these do you especially look forward to?
http://www.joyfulheart.com/forums/index.php?showtopic=140

21:4 Every cause of sorrow shall be past and unremembered forever. Hallelujah! (7:15; 1 Corinthians 15:26, 54; Isaiah 25:8; 35:10; 65:19).

21:6 "To the thirsty ... the water of life without payment" (Isaiah 55:1; Revelation 22:17; John 4:10-14; 7:37-39). This reference is the source of the '70s praise chorus "Come to the Waters" by Marsha Stevens.

Q2. Read Revelation 21:6; 22:17; and Isaiah 55:1-3. What does the "water of life" represent here and in 22:1? In what sense is it a "free gift" (22:17). In what ways should "the Spirit and the Bride" (22:17) extend that invitation in your community?
http://www.joyfulheart.com/forums/index.php?showtopic=141

21:7 "To him who conquers." Here is another in the line of promises to all true Christians, offered at the ending of each of the letters to the seven churches (chapters 2-3). Those who conquer are those who are brave in the face of persecution and faithful unto death (12:11) and have not denied their Lord.

21:8 "The cowardly, the faithless ..." Those who deny their Lord face the same punishment as the unbelievers of the earth (Matthew 10:22, 32; 13:21; 2 Timothy 2:12; Mark 8:35).

"Fornicators ... liars." If we adopt the world's standards instead of our Messiah's, we share the world's fate (18:4). Many Christians used to partake in these sins, but we have been washed, cleansed, and forgiven (1 Corinthians 6:9-11).

21:9 "One of the seven angels" (17:1). The one who introduced the scarlet Prostitute of Babylon now introduces the pure Bride of the Lamb. What a contrast!

"I will show you the Bride, the wife of the Lamb" (see notes on 21:2 above). Christ is not married to a city any more than the Church is married to a Lamb. These are symbols of spiritual realities. The greatness, glory, and grandeur of God's Church are described using symbolism of a bride. In Ephesians 5:27 we see the Church "in splendor, without a spot or wrinkle or anything of the kind – yes, so that she may be holy and without blemish" (NRSV). In Revelation 21 she is pictured as a perfect city.

21:12 "Twelve gates" represent the 12 tribes of Israel. Here is the basis of the gospel song, "Twelve Gates to the City, Hallelujah."

21:14 "Twelve foundations" represent the 12 apostles. The gates and the foundations are the prototype of God's Old and New Testament churches, respectively. This is the same symbolism as the 24 elders (4:4).

21:15 "Measuring rod" (11:1; Ezekiel 40:3; Zechariah 2:1).

21:16 "Foursquare" (KJV, NRSV) or "square" (NIV), that is, perfect.

"12,000 stadia," if you were to take it literally, would be about 1,400 miles in each dimension – a giant cube. A cube was the shape of the holy of holies of Solomon's temple (1 Kings 6:20), the place of divine presence. The dimensions are not to be taken literally or visually, however, but symbolically (12 x 1000).

21:17 "Wall, 144 cubits," or about 216 feet. If you take this literally it is all out of proportion for a city so immense, but it is symbolic: 12 x 12 = 144.

21:18 "The city was pure gold, clear as glass." Gold is not clear, no matter how pure. Again we are to look symbolically, not visually. Gold = great value. Clear glass = purity.

21:19 "Adorned with every jewel." The twelve stones correspond with most of the stones in the high priest's breastplate (Exodus 28:17-20).

21:22 "Its temple is the Lord God and the Lamb" (7:15; Ezekiel 40-46). Symbol has now given way to reality. The inhabitants don't need a place of worship or sacrifice, for the Object of all worship is present and the great Sacrifice himself is there.

21:23 "No need of sun or moon." (Isaiah 60:1-3, 19; Zechariah 14:7). The Shekinah presence of God is enough. (See John 1:4, 9, 14.)

21:24 "The kings of the earth shall bring their glory into it." This is the fulfillment of an Old Testament prophetic theme (Isaiah 60:3-5, 11-14; 66:12).

21:25 "Its gates shall never be shut" (Isaiah 60:11). There is no enemy to protect against or exclude.

21:27 "Nothing unclean shall enter." Finally, "Jerusalem" shall be a holy city (Joel 3:17; Isaiah 35: 8-10; 52:11; Ezekiel 44:9).

21:27 "The Lamb's book of life" (3:5; 13:8; 20:12; 20:15; Philippians 4:3; Luke 10:20). This concludes an Old Testament theme of those who are recorded for life (Exodus 32:32; Psalm 69:28; Isaiah 4:3; Ezekiel 13:9; Daniel 12:1).

Q3. (Revelation 21:9-27) John's vision of the Holy City is obviously strongly symbolic. But the Holy City pictures "the bride, the wife of the Lamb" (21:9-10; 21:2). What does John's vision of the Holy City tell us about the way that Jesus looks at his Church?
http://www.joyfulheart.com/forums/index.php?showtopic=142

Q4. Three times in these two chapters, John stresses that those who continue to practice sin will not enter. Read Revelation 21:8, 27; 22:14-15; and 1 Corinthians 6:9-11. What things in these passages point to salvation by the grace of God rather than mere salvation by right living? In what way is holy living important to salvation? Why is holy living important to God?
http://www.joyfulheart.com/forums/index.php?showtopic=143

The River of Life (22:1-6)

The theme of the river that flows from the God's throne is the focus of an old Gospel hymn by Robert Lowry (1864), "Shall We Gather at the River?" The refrain goes:

"Yes, we'll gather at the river, the beautiful, the beautiful river,
Gather with the saints at the river, that flows by the throne of God."

22:1 "The river of the water of life ... from the throne" (7:17; 21:6; 22:17; Genesis 2:10; Ezekiel 47:1-12; Zechariah 14:8; Joel 3:18).

22:2 "The tree of life" is nourished by the water of life. This refers back to the Garden of Eden's promise before the Fall (Genesis 3:22-24; Ezekiel 47:12). The promise of this fruit is the promise of eternal life (2:7; 22:14).

"Leaves ... for the healing of the nations" (Ezekiel 47:12). Here is a promise of complete relief from physical disease and suffering, as well as peace between peoples.

22:4 "They shall see his face." Final intimacy is allowed in heaven's holiness. Moses was allowed only to see "God's backside" (Exodus 33:20-23). To see God in an unholy state would mean instant death (Genesis 32:30; 16:13; Exodus 24:10-11; 33:20;

8. We Shall See His Face (chapters 21-22)

Judges 13:21-22; Isaiah 6:5). But this is the promise to the pure in heart (Matthew 5:8), and its hope brings purity to our lives (1 John 3:2-3).

Jesus Is Coming (22:7-21)

22:7 "Behold, I am coming soon" (1:3; 3:11; 22:12) . We must be ready.

22:10 "Do not seal up the words" (compare Daniel 8:26).

22:11 "Let the evildoer still do evil" (Daniel 12:10; Ezekiel 3:27). There will come a time when it will be too late for repentance. At the present time the invitation of 22:17 is still open.

22:12 "My reward is with me, to repay according to everyone's work" (Isaiah 40:10; 62:11). Judgment, justice at last. God gives rebellious man only so much rope. There is a day He will pull in the line.

22:14 "Wash their robes" – that is, repent and turn to Jesus for forgiveness and cleansing. (7:14). Verses 11 and 14-15 show the contrast, the eventual division of the righteous and the wicked.

22:14 "Enter the city by the gates" recalls John 10:1-2.

22:16 "This testimony for the churches." We return now to the seven churches that have not been mentioned since chapter 3.

"I am the root and the offspring of David" – that is, the true Messiah (5:5; Isaiah 11:1, 10; Romans 1:3).

"The bright morning star" (Numbers 24:17; Revelation 2:28). The morning star is a promise that the long night of tribulation is all but over and that the new, unending Day is about to dawn.

22:17 "Come!" This is a final invitation from the Holy Spirit and the Church, echoed by those who take heed and quench their thirst with the water of life. There is still time to come, but it cannot be counted on to remain long.

"Take the water of life without price" (21:6; Isaiah 55:1). Some people see in Revelation only harsh, unremitting judgment. But the vision ends with grace offered freely to all. Grace is seen as the only way to life. Revelation does not teach salvation by works. But it does teach the necessity of repudiating any other way of life except embracing Jesus, who alone supplies grace and salvation.

22:18 The curse as stated applies specifically to this Book of Revelation, not to the 66 books of the canonical Scripture.

22:20 "He who testifies to these things..." – Jesus. Revelation purports to be a revelation from Jesus Christ himself, as seen and recorded by John (1:1-2). To ignore the message of Revelation is to ignore the teaching of Jesus himself to his Church.

22:20 "Come, Lord Jesus." A promise and a response from Christ's people. If we love the world and the things in the world (1 John 2:15), we want to put off His return. But the Church and the earth have groaned too long under bondage, decay, persecution, death (Romans 8:18-25). Let us be ready, let us be those "who have loved his appearing" (2 Timothy 4:8). "Come, Lord Jesus" is the equivalent of the ancient Aramaic watchwords which close 1 Corinthians (16:22) – "Maranatha!"

Q5. (Revelation 22:20) If you were convinced that Jesus Christ would return in your lifetime, how would it affect your life? What would you do differently than you do now?
http://www.joyfulheart.com/forums/index.php?showtopic=144

22:21 "The grace of the Lord Jesus be with God's people." Revelation is terrible in its vision of judgment, but rich in its offer of and appreciation of grace. Jesus the Redeemer is seen as the Lamb of God (chapter 5; John 1:29), the Lamb that God himself sent to die for our sins and take them away from us.

Knowing what we know, we will either fall down and worship him or turn away and face his judgments. My prayer for you, my friend, is that you come to know this Lamb. That your name is written in his Book of Life. And that you receive the grace of God that rests upon his people.

Prayer

Father, these chapters paint such a scene of peace, of rest, of resolution, of reward and happiness. You have promises for us to encourage us while we experience persecutions and hardships. And we look forward to that time when we can be so much in your immediate presence that we are fully immersed in you. In Jesus' name we hope and pray. Amen.

Appendix 1: Questions for Group Participants

If you're working with a class or small group, feel free to duplicate the following handouts in this Appendices 1 and 2 at no additional charge. If you'd like to print 8-1/2" x 11" or A4 sheets, you can download the free Participant Guide handout sheets at: **www.jesuswalk.com/revelation/revelation-lesson-handouts.pdf**

Discussion Questions

You'll find 4 to 6 questions for each lesson. Each question may include several sub-questions. These are designed to get group members engaged in discussion of the key points of the passage. If you're running short of time, feel free to skip questions or portions of questions.

Charts

For many lessons there are charts which will aid in study. It's best to distribute most of the charts a week ahead of time (according to the schedule below) so people have a chance to read the lessons and fill out the charts before your group meets. It's best to download the set from the Internet so they'll copy easily on standard size paper.

1. Christ in the Midst of the Lampstands (Rev. 1)
2. Letters to the Seven Churches (Rev. 2-3)
   7 Churches Comparison chart
3. The Lion That Is the Lamb (Rev 4-5)
4. The 144,000 (Rev. 6-10)
   7 Seals chart
   7 Trumpets chart
   Parallelism chart
5. By the Blood of the Lamb (Rev. 11-13)
   7 Mystic Figures chart
6. Alas, Babylon!(Rev. 14-18)
   Visions of Final Judgment chart
   7 Bowls chart
7. The Millennium (Rev. 19-20)
   Chronologies of the Millennium and Christ's Return chart
8. We Shall See His Face (Rev. 21-22)

1. Christ in the Midst of the Lampstands (chapter 1)

Purpose and Theme of the Book of Revelation

The purpose of the Revelation is to jolt those Christians who are compromising with idolatry out of their spiritual anesthesia so that they will perceive the spiritual danger they are in and repent (Beale). It is also designed to comfort and encourage the faithful, witnessing church in its struggle against the forces of evil. Assurance is given that: God sees their tears (7:17; 21:4); their prayers rule the world! (8:3-4); death ushers them into a glorious heaven (14:13; 20:4); their final victory is assured (15:2); their Christ lives and reigns forever, who governs the world in the interest of His church (5:7-8); and that He is coming again to take his people to Himself (chapters. 21-22). The theme of the book is the victory of Christ and of His church over the dragon (Satan) and his helpers. The theme is stated in 17:14:

> "They will make war on the Lamb, and the Lamb will conquer them, for He is Lord of lords and King of kings, and those with Him are called and chosen and faithful."

Interpretation

Historically there have been four major divisions of interpretation (with many variations):

1. The **preterite**–everything has already been fulfilled.
2. The **historical**–the predictions are in the process of fulfillment.
3. The **futurist**–all predictions are in the future.
4. The **spiritual**–the events described are only symbols of spiritual realities and struggles, without any literal or historical application.

John was told, "Now write what you see, what is and what is to take place hereafter" (1:19). After the letters to the seven churches he is told, "Come up hither, and I will show you what must take place after this" (4:1). As the author considers the text, he finds it necessary sometimes to hold the preterite view (this was fulfilled in the first century or shortly thereafter); sometimes the historical view (this was fulfilled in the middle ages, or is in the process of fulfillment); sometimes the futurist view (this is still yet to come); or perhaps even the spiritual view (that these events are symbols of spiritual realities and struggles).

Appendix 1: Questions for Group Participants

Principles of Interpretation

1. The Revelation is rooted in **contemporaneous events and circumstances**. Its symbols should be interpreted in light of the conditions which prevailed when the book was written.
2. Revelation shares a characteristic of Bible prophets, in that **contemporary historical events** are seen as a **type of, or a prelude to, the great Day of the Lord** in the latter days. Often they do this without a chronological distinction between the two.
3. **John is an artist in words and symbols**. We are to look for the meaning conveyed by each symbol in that symbol itself. It doesn't really matter whether or not the symbols can be visualized or reconciled.
4. **Be hesitant to speculate** which, if any, *current* events, nations, or political figures are referred to in Revelation. The history of interpretation is littered with hundreds of mistaken identities. Rather look for the basic structure of events and principles of faith and action for Christians in the End Times.
5. **Be reluctant to superimpose upon Revelation a preconceived system of interpretation** (that is, pre-, post-, a-millennial, or pre-, mid, or post-tribulation rapture). In this study we'll consider these various alternatives. The time to synthesize the *whole* teaching of the Bible about the End Times is after we have carefully analyzed each portion on its own terms.
6. Revelation may not be **a simple chronology of events from chapters 4 through 22**; rather a **series of visions which may parallel each other** chronologically, but which emphasize different aspects of divine truth. This view is called "parallelism".
7. **We can learn much from Revelation, even though there are parts we do not understand**. Consider yourself a student of the book, not a master of it. God will reveal some of the hidden parts of Revelation to Christians only when we need to know them. Until then, all our speculations are a waste of time and can get in the way of learning.

Q1. Revelation is written to encourage and strengthen a church facing intense persecution. Why is the theme of testimony and witness so important to that purpose? How is Jesus as the "faithful witness" (1:5) supposed to encourage us? Why are we afraid to be clear witnesses in a culture where we aren't persecuted?

Q2. What does 1:8 tell us about the Father? The Father is the speaker here in 1:8 and in 21:6. But Jesus is the speaker in 1:17 and 22:12-13. What is the significance of this for our understanding of who Jesus is?

Q3. In what countries are Christians presently experiencing tribulation or persecution for the faith? How can the Book of Revelation be a comfort and encouragement to them?

Q4. The vision of Christ among the lampstands (1:12-20) is much different than the Carpenter-Teacher who walked the roads of Galilee and Judea. Why? What overall emotions is this vision of Jesus among the lampstands designed to evoke in the reader? Why is this understanding of Jesus important to a balanced faith?

Q5. What is the significance of the exalted Jesus walking among the lampstands? What does this teach us about the church? What does it teach us about Jesus?

Note: Distribute the 7 Churches Comparison Chart today so people can study for next week.

2. Letters to the Seven Churches (chapters 2-3)

Q1. How can a local congregation lose its "first love" for Jesus? What are the signs of genuine love for Jesus in worship and ministry? How does the lack of love show up? How can a congregation regain this love?

Q2. Why would loosening of sexual standards to conform to the prevailing morals of the culture be destructive of vital Christian faith and witness? How has your culture tended to take the edge off your own Christian moral convictions or forced you to be quiet about them?

Q3. Why do you think the religious compromise required by participating in heathen religious practices in the trade guilds was so spiritually destructive? What compromises do twenty-first century Christians struggle with? Let's not settle for trite legalisms about drinking and smoking. What are the real compromises that dilute vital Christianity?

Q4. Why are so many churches a "hotbed of apathy"? (Don't rag on other denominations!) How can we combat spiritual apathy and an insipid witness in ourselves?

Q5. Summarize the lessons of this chapter. What are the churches criticized for? What are they praised for? How should these observations shape the twenty-first century Church?

Note: No need to distribute charts for next week's lesson.

3. The Lion That Is the Lamb (chapters 4-5)

Q1. Many Christian hymns, songs, and choruses come from Revelation chapters 4 and 5. Which can you think of?

Q2. These chapters contain many insights into worship that have been adopted by the Christian Church. What do you learn about Christian worship from chapters 4 and 5? Don't miss the basics. Your list might include 20 elements and concepts of worship – or more.

Q3. (Revelation 5:9, 12) *What made Jesus so worthy* of opening the scroll and thus bringing history to its consummation? Why was this act so noteworthy and praiseworthy?

Q4. (Revelation 5:10) How can our destiny as believers include reigning? In what sense could we reign? In what sense do we serve as priests? In what sense are we a kingdom?

Q5. (Revelation 5:13) What is the significance of the same quality of worship being offered to both God the Father and Jesus Christ the Son? What does this tell us about their relationship to each other? Their relationship to us?

Note: Distribute so people will be able to study them for next week these items:

1. 7 Seals Chart
2. 7 Trumpets Chart
3. Parallelism Chart

Appendix 1: Questions for Group Participants

4. The 144,000 (chapters 6-10)

Q1. (Revelation 6) Who initiates this great storm of destruction represented by the Seven Seals? Against whom is it directed? Is it just?

Q2. (Revelation 6:9-11) What do we learn about the Church from what is revealed in the Fifth Seal? Where are these "souls" at the time of this scene? What does their proximity to the altar signify? Why were they killed? Why do they ask for vengeance? Is that a Christian prayer? What does the white robe represent? What do we learn from their instruction to "wait a little longer"?

Q3. (Revelation 7:1-4) There's disagreement about exactly who the 144,000 represent. Let's not debate that, but look deeper. From 7:1-4 what do we learn about God? Read Ezekiel 9, then answer: What is this seal supposed to do for the 144,000? (Please wait to consider 14:1-5 until we get there, okay?)

Q4. (Revelation 7:9-18). From this passage what do we learn about the kind of people who make up the "great multitude" before the throne? Let's *not* debate whether they are the 144,000 or not. But what is their origin? What does their spirit within them cause them to do? What does the first verse of the song "Amazing Grace" have to do with 7:14?

Q5. (Revelation 10:1-9) What is bitter about what you've read in Revelation 6 through 10? What is sweet? Why do we tend to reject what is hard for us to understand?

Note: Distribute so participants can study them for next week the 7 Mystic Figures chart.

5. By The Blood of the Lamb (chapters 11-13)

Q1. (11:3-12) Interpreters disagree upon the identity of the Two Witnesses, but they are certainly strong and brave. What positive characteristics do you see in their actions that we should emulate in our day? What is their reward?

Q2. (12:1-17) The vision of the woman and the dragon is heavily symbolic, but comprehensible when you take care to understand. In your own words, what does this vision tell us about the cosmic battle in Jesus' day and in our own? What comfort should we disciples draw from this passage?

Q3. Revelation 12:11 could be considered a theme verse for the book. What does it mean? Who is overcome? In what sense do we have victory if we die in the process? What does the "blood of the Lamb" have to do with this? How does loving our lives prevent spiritual victory today? (See Luke 14:25-27; Matthew 10:37-39.)

Q4. (13:1-18, optional) The two beasts belong to the period of the ascendancy of the Antichrist at the very end of the Last Days. Together with 2 Thessalonians 2:1-12, summarize what have you learned about the Antichrist and the False Prophet.

Gospel Age ("Tribulation")	"Great Tribulation"
Church trampled 42 months, 2 witnesses prophecy 1260 days (Revelation 11:2-3)	2 witnesses dead, 3-1/2 days (Revelation 11:9)
Woman in wilderness, church protected to declare gospel, 1260 days. 1X, 2X 1/2X (Revelation 12:6, 14)	War on offspring; beast: authority; church decimated by persecution, 42 months (Revelation 13:5-7)
Mystery of lawlessness at work but restrained (2 Thessalonians 2:7)	The lawless one will be revealed (2 Thessalonians 2:8)
Spirit of antichrist (1 John 2:18b)	Antichrist prevails (1 John 2:18a)
Sacrifice and offering (Daniel 9:27a)	Abomination in temple, desolator (Daniel 9:27b)
Power of holy people (Daniel 12:7a; 1X, 2X, 1/2X).	After shattering of power of holy people. Time after abomination, 1290 days. Total = 1335 days (Daniel 12:7b, 11-12)
	"Little Horn" wears out saints 1X, 2X 1/2X (Daniel 7:21-25)

Appendix 1: Questions for Group Participants

Note: Distribute in advance so people can study Revelation 14-18 for next week:

1. Visions of Final Judgment chart
2. 7 Bowls chart

6. Alas, Babylon! (chapters 14-18)

Q1. (14:3-5) In what ways do the 144,000 provide an ideal for all Christians to emulate?

Q2. (14:10-11) Why is everlasting punishment so difficult for us Christians to accept? In what ways might eternal punishment be considered just punishment?

Q3. (15:3-4) We see singing and praise in heaven before the throne a number of times in Revelation (4:8, 11; 5:9-10, 12-13; 7:12; 11:17-18; 15:3-4; 19:1-3). What do you learn about appropriate worship from studying these songs? Do you recognize any contemporary songs that seem similar to these?

Q4. (18:4) We Christians are instructed to be "in the world" but not "of the world" (John 17:15-19). One interpretation has been to be hermits, ascetics, to distance ourselves from the political process, and to adopt stringent dress and behavior codes. Another interpretation is to be "salt and light" (Matthew 5:13-16) in the world so that we might bring about cleansing and change through God's spirit. Where do you think the balance lies? How and when should we fulfill the command, "Come out of her, my people, so that you will not share in her sins...."?

Note: No charts need to be distributed in advance this week, but read carefully Revelation 19-20.

Appendix 1: Questions for Group Participants

7. The Millennium (chapters 19-20)

Q1. (19:7-9) These verses draw together two themes from Scripture – (1) God's people as his betrothed Bride and (2) the feast of all God's people in heaven. When you meditate on these themes, how are you both admonished and encouraged?

Q2. (19:16) What are the implications of Christ's title: "King of kings and Lord of lords" for your life? For the everyday world that surrounds you?

Q3. (20:11-12) Why is this awesome scene of judgment so frightening? Why do people seem to resist the idea of a final judgment?

Q4. (20:12-15) Here is a serious question for each of us – not one we should respond to with pat answers. What assurance do you have that your name is written in the Book of Life?

Note: Distribute with today's lesson one chart to be discussed in class, the final Chronologies of the Millennium and Christ's Return chart

8. We Shall See His Face (chapters 21-22)

Q1. (21:3-5) What is the significance of the fact that in heaven "God himself will be with them"? Why can the promises in 21:4 only be fulfilled in heaven? Which of these do you especially look forward to?

Q2. Read Revelation 21:6; 22:17; and Isaiah 55:1-3. What does the "water of life" represent here and in 22:1? In what sense is it a "free gift" (22:17). In what ways should "the Spirit and the Bride" (22:17) extend that invitation in your community?

Q3. (Revelation 21:9-27) John's vision of the Holy City is obviously strongly symbolic. But the Holy City pictures "the bride, the wife of the Lamb" (21:9-10; 21:2). What does John's vision of the Holy City tell us about the way that Jesus looks at his Church?

Q4. Three times in these two chapters, John stresses that those who continue to practice sin will not enter. Read Revelation 21:8, 27; 22:14-15; and 1 Corinthians 6:9-11. What things in these passages point to salvation by the grace of God rather than mere salvation by right living? In what way is holy living important to salvation? Why is holy living important to God?

Q5. (Revelation 22:20) If you were convinced that Jesus Christ would return in your lifetime, how would it affect your life? What would you do differently than you do now?

Note: No charts are to be distributed with today's lesson. This concludes our study of Revelation.

Appendix 2: Charts

The charts that follow may be duplicated for class or small group participants at no charge:

1. 7 Churches Comparison chart (for Lesson 2, two sheets to be taped together. Distribute at the conclusion of Lesson 1)
2. 7 Seals chart (for Lesson 4, distribute at the conclusion of Lesson 3)
3. 7 Trumpets chart (for Lesson 4, distribute at the conclusion of Lesson 3)
4. Parallelism chart (for Lesson 4, two sheets to be taped together, distribute at the conclusion of Lesson 3)
5. 7 Mystic Figures chart (for Lesson 5, distribute at the conclusion of Lesson 4)
6. Visions of Final Judgment chart (for Lesson 6, distribute at the conclusion of Lesson 5)
7. 7 Bowls chart (for Lesson 6, distribute at the conclusion of Lesson 5)
8. Chronologies of the Millennium and Christ's Return chart (for Lesson 7, do not distribute ahead of time, but is for classroom discussion during Lesson 7)

Comparison Chart — Letters to the Seven Churches of Revelation

	Ephesus (2:1-7)	Smyrna (2:8-11)	Pergamum (2:12-17)	Thyatira (2:18-29)	Sardis (3:1-6)
Portrayal of Jesus	7 stars in hand Walks among lampstands				
Praise for the Church	Patient endurance Toil, sound doctrine (hates Nicolaitans)				
Criticism of the Church	Abandoned earlier love				
Exhortation: A. Correction/ Encouragement	Remember, repent, do earlier works				
B. Penalty/ Reward	Lampstand can be removed				
Promises to Overcomers	Eat of the tree of life				
General Admonition	"He who has an ear, let him hear what the Spirit says to the churches."				

The Seven Seals (Revelation 6)

1		White horse Bow Crown Conquering	6:1-2
2		Bright red horse Great sword Take peace from the earth	6:3-4
3		Black horse Balance Famine	6:5-6
4		Pale horse Death and Hades 1/4 of earth Death	6:7-8
5		Souls of martyrs under the altar "How long?"	6:9-11
6		Signs in heavens Sun, moon, stars, sky Day of Wrath	6:12-17
7		Silence	8:1

The Seven Trumpets (Revelation 8-11)

#		Description	Verses
1		Earth burned 1/3 destroyed	8:7
2		Sea to blood 1/3 sea, 1/3 fish 1/3 ships	8:8-9
3		Water poisoned "Wormwood" Star 1/3 water bitter	8:10-11
4		Sun, moon, stars 1/3 darkened	8:12
5		Locusts Torture 5 months from bottomless pit	9:1-12
6		Cavalry host kills 1/3 4 angels, 200 million horses	9:13-21
		Little Scroll eaten Bitter — Sweet	10:1-11
		Two Witnesses prophecy 1260 days, slain 3-1/2 days, resurrection, rapture	11:1-14
7		Consummation: Christ reigns Kingdoms > Christ	11:15-19

Copyright © 2011, Ralph F. Wilson pastor@joyfulheart.com *Revelation: Discipleship Lessons* www.jesuswalk.com/books/revelation.htm

Appendix 2: Charts

Parallelism in Revelation

Print this out as a single page at www.jesuswalk.com/revelation/parallelism.pdf You'll find all sorts of theories of how Revelation fits together. Some see the series of 7 seals, 7 trumpets, and 7 bowls chronologically following one after another. The interpretation I think works best is a partial parallelism as suggested below. You'll see many parallels, but some don't fit so well. Certainly, parallelism has some weaknesses – but so do all the other views.

Matthew 24	7 Seals (Rev 6)	7 Trumpets (Rev 8-9, 11)	7 Bowls (Rev 16)
Many come in my name (5)	1. White Horse (false messiah?), conquering (1-2)		
Wars & rumors of wars (6-7a)	2. Red Horse, war (3-4)		
Famines & earthquakes (7b-8)	3. Black horse, famine (5-6)		
	4. Pale horse, pestilence, famine, death (7-8)		
Tribulation of the church, many fall (9-11)	5. Heavenly vision of martyrs (9-11)		
Love grow cold, endure, gospel preached (12-14)			
Desolating sacrilege in holy place (15)			
Feeling judgments on Jerusalem (16-20)			
Great tribulation (21-22)			
		1. Hail and fire (8:7)	1. Sores (2)
		2. Seas turn to blood (8:8-9)	2. Sea like blood (3)

		3. Wormwood, bitter (8:10-11)	3. Fresh water turns to blood (4)
Sun dark, moon dark, stars fall, heavenly bodies shaken (29)	6. Earthquake, sun dark, moon blood, stars fall, sky rolled up, earth moves (12-14)	4. Sun, moon, stars darkened (8:12)	4. Sun scorches people (8-9) 5. Darkness on beast's kingdom
Nations mourn (30a)	Ungodly leaders hide in caves, cry for fear of wrath of the Lamb (15-17)		
	Sealing of 144,000 for protection (chap 7)		
	7. Silence (8:1)		
		5. Locusts torture unbelievers, but not believers (9:1-12)	
		6. 200 million cavalry kills 1/3 (9:13-19)	6. Nations assemble, battle of Armageddon (12-16)
Son of Man on the clouds with great power and glory, trumpet call, gathers his elect—rapture (30b)		7. Kingdoms are Christ's, dead judged, servants rewarded, destroyer destroyed (11:15-19)	7. "It is done." Lightning, thunder, earthquake, Babylon falls, hailstones, cursing God (16-21). Marriage Supper, judgment (chapters 19-20)

Copyright © 2011, Ralph F. Wilson <pastor@joyfulheart.com>. All rights reserved. Excerpt from *Book of Revelation: Discipleship Lessons* (JesusWalk, 2011), www.jesuswalk.com/books/revelation.htm

Appendix 2: Charts

The Seven Mystic Figures (Revelation 12-14)

#		Figure	Reference
1		The woman with child	12:1-2, 6, 13-16
2		Red Dragon, 7 heads, 10 horns, 7 diadems on heads. = Devil = Satan = Ancient serpent	12:3-4
3		Male child	12:5
4		Archangel Michael	12:7-12
5		Beast from the Sea. 10 horns, 7 heads, 10 diadems on heads (= Antichrist)	13:1-10
6		Beast from the Earth. 2 horns, like lamb, spoke like dragon. Number is 666	13:11-18
7		Lamb and the 144,000 on Mt. Zion	14:1-5

Copyright © 2011, Ralph F. Wilson pastor@joyfulheart.com Revelation: Discipleship Lessons www.jesuswalk.com/books/revelation.htm

Visions of Final Judgment (Revelation 14:6-20)

	Eternal Gospel Worship God	First Angel	14:6-7
	Fallen, fallen is Babylon the Great	Second Angel	14:8
	God's wrath Judgment of fire and brimstone	Third Angel	14:9-11
	Reap the harvest of the earth		14:14-16
	Reap the vintage of the earth		14:17-20

The Seven Bowls of God's Wrath (Revelation 16)

#		Description	Reference
1		Foul and evil sores	16:2
2		Sea becomes as blood of a corpse	16:3
3		Fresh water becomes blood	16:4-7
4		Sun scorches men with fire	16:8-9
5		Darkness on the throne of the beast. Torment.	16:10-11
6		River Euphrates dries up. Armies march to Battle of Armageddon.	16:12-16 17:7-18
7		Great earthquake. Babylon and major cities destroyed. Hailstones.	16:17-21 Ch. 18

Copyright © 2011, Ralph F. Wilson pastor@joyfulheart.com *Revelation: Discipleship Lessons* www.jesuswalk.com/books/revelation.htm

Chronologies of the Millennium and Christ's Return
Theories of the Order of Events

Great Tribulation — The "7 year" period marking the rise of the Antichrist, increase of evil, persecution of Christians (Matthew 24:21, 29; 2 Thessalonians 2:1-12; Revelation 7:14;), just prior to Christ's return in glory (Matthew 24:30-31; Acts 1:11). One's theory of the time of the rapture is described as pre-trib, mid-trib, or post-trib.

Rapture — (from Latin *raptus*, "snatch away"), the catching up of Christians to meet Christ in the End Time (Matthew 24:29-31; 1 Corinthians 15:51-52; 1 Thessalonians 4:13-18; 2 Thessalonians 2:1).

Millennium — "1,000 year" period of Christ's earthly reign, during which time Satan is bound (Revelation 20:1-6). One's theory of the timing of Christ's return is described as pre-millennial or post-millennial (before or after the millennium). Amillennialists believe the millennium is not a literal period time, but coincides with the Church Age.

Church Age — The period of time the Church has to declare the Gospel before Christ's return (Matthew 24:14; Luke 21:24; Romans 11:25)

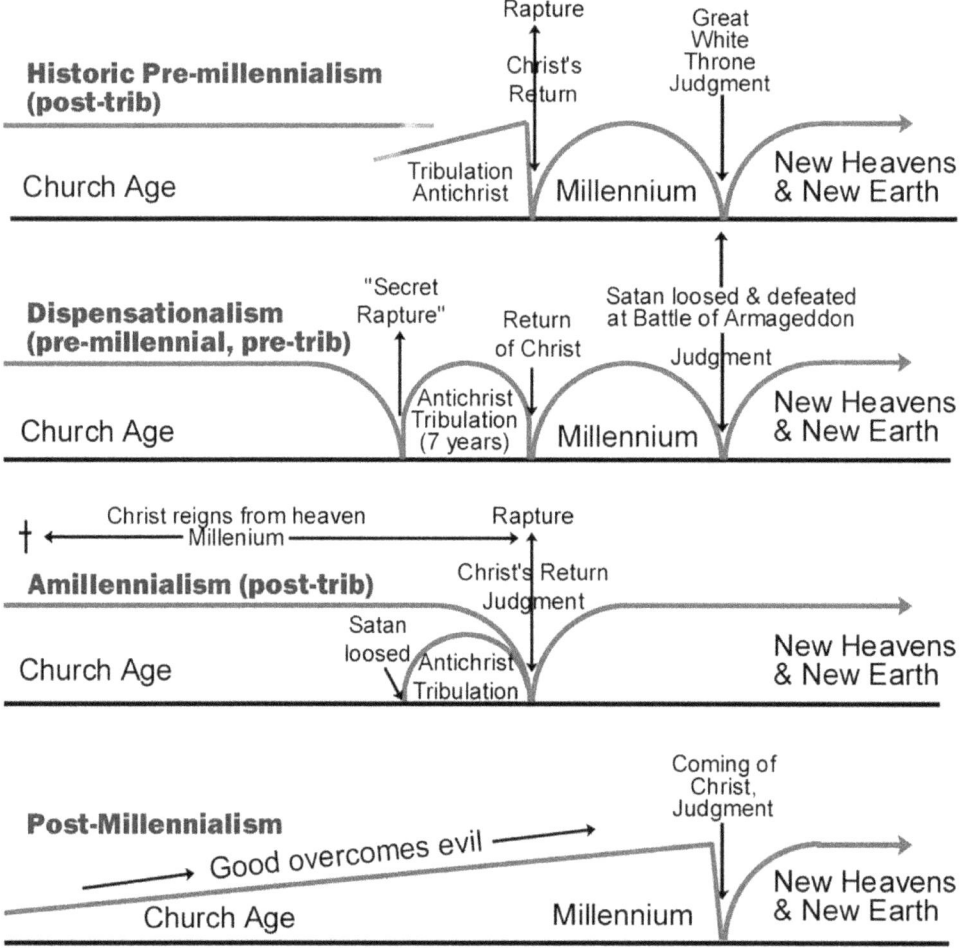

Copyright © 2011, Ralph F. Wilson pastor@joyfulheart.com *Revelation: Discipleship Lessons* www.jesuswalk.com/revelation

Appendix 3. Songs and Hymns Based on Revelation

The book of Revelation has inspired many hymns and songs over the years. The throne-room scene in Rev 4-5 has spawned a number of "Worthy" songs. Also the vision of the conquering King in Rev 19, the judgment in Rev 20, and the vision of heaven in Rev 21-22 have been particularly rich. "Crossing Jordan" and the "River of Life" are themes found in many songs. I haven't tried to be comprehensive here, just collect some of the songs that seem more popular.

1:5-6	"I Will Praise Him" ("Praise the Lamb for sinners slain...."), by Margaret Jenkins Harris (1898)
1:7	"Every Eye Shall See," by William J. and Gloria Gaither (1980, Gaither Music Company)
2:17	"New Name in Glory," by C. Austin Miles (1910)
4-5	"How Great Is Our God" ("the Lion and the Lamb"... "beginning and the end"), by Christ Tomlin, Ed Cash, Jesse Reeves (2004, worshiptogether.com)
4:8	"Holy, Holy, Holy," words: Reginald Heber (1826); music: "Nicaea, John B. Dykes (1861)
4:8; 5:12	"Revelation Song" ("Holy, holy, holy ... Worthy is the Lamb") by Jennie Lee Riddle (2004, Gateway Create)
4:11	"Thou Art Worthy," by Pauline Michael Mills (1963, 1975, Fred Bock Music Co.)
5:5	"It's Rising Up," by Martin Smith and Matt Redman (1995, Thankyou Music)
5:11	"O, for a Thousand Tongues to Sing," words: Charles Wesley (1739), music: "Azmon," Carl G. Gläser (1828)
5:12	"Worthy," by Rich Cook (1977, John T. Benson Publishing Co.)
5:12	"Worthy Is the Lamb," by Robert C. Clatterbuck (1988, Hope Publishing Company)
5:12	"Worthy Is the Lamb," by Don Wyrtzen (1973, Singspiration Music / ASCAP)

5:12	"Worthy Is the Lamb," by Darlene Zschech (2000, Hillsong Publishing)
5:23	"Agnus Dei," by Michael W. Smith (1990, Sony / ATV Milene Music)
5:12	"I Will Praise Him" ("praise the Lamb for sinners slain"), words and music by Margaret J. Harris (1898)
5:13	"Lamb of Glory," by Greg Nelson and Phill McHugh (1982 River Oaks Music / Shepherd's Fold Music)
7:9	"Behold a Host," by Hans Adolph Brorson (1760) translated by Gracia Grindal, traditional Norwegian folk melody, ca. 1600)
7:14	"Are You Washed in the Blood," words and music: Elisha A. Hoffman (1878)
7:14	"There's Power in the Blood," words and music: Lewis E. Jones (1899)
12:11	"Victory in Jesus," words and music by Eugene M. Bartlett (1939, E.M. Bartlett, renewed)
12:11	"We Shall Overcome," African American spiritual
14:3	"Redeemed, How I Love to Proclaim It," words: Fanny J. Crosby (1882), music: William J. Kirkpatrick
14:15	"Come, Ye Thankful People, Come" (For the Lord our God shall come, and shall take His harvest home..."), words: Henry Alford (1844), music: "St. George's Windsor," George J. Elvey (1858)
14:19	"Battle Hymn of the Republic" ("trampling out the vintage where the grapes of wrath are stored..."), words: Julia Ward Howe (1861), music: "John Brown's Body," possibly by John William Steffe
15:3	"I Will Sing the Wondrous Story" ("...gathered by the crystal sea"), words: Frances H. Rowley (1886), music: Peter P. Bilhorn (1886)
15:4	"We Will Glorify," by Twila Paris (1982, New Spring)
15:4	"Holy, Holy," by Jimmy Owens (1979, Bud John Songs, Inc.)
17:14	"Jesus Is Lord of All," by William J. and Gloria Gaither (1973, William J. Gaither)

Appendix 3. Songs and Hymns Based on Revelation 111

19:16	"All Hail, King Jesus," by Dave Moody (1981, Dayspring Music, LLC)
19:1	"Alleluia," by Jerry Sinclair (1972, Manna Music, Inc.)
19:1	"Sing Hallelujah," by Linda Stassen (1974, Linda Stassen, New songs Ministries)
19:12	"Crown Him with Many Crowns," words: Matthew Bridges and Godfrey Thring (1874), music: "Diademata," George J. Elvey (1868)
19:12	"All Hail the Power of Jesus' Name," words: Edward Perronet (1779), music: "Coronation," Oliver Holden (1793)
19:13	"Jesus, Name Above All Names," by Naida Hearn (1974, 1978, Scripture in Song)
20:12	"When the Roll Is Called Up Yonder," words and music: James M. Black (1893)
21:1	"Walk in Jerusalem, Just Like John" ("I Want to Be Ready"), African American spiritual
21:2	"When We All Get to Heaven," words: Eliza E. Hewitt (1898), music: Emily D. Wilson
21:2	"When the Saints Go Marching In," African American spiritual, made popular by Louis Armstrong
21:2	"The Holy City" ("Jerusalem, Jerusalem, lift up your voice and sing), words: Frederick E. Weatherly (1892), music: Michael Maybrick
21:2	That Beautiful Land," words: Mrs. F.A.F. Wood White (1889), Music: J.M. Hagan
21:2	"Marching to Zion" (..."beautiful city of God"), words: Isaac Watts (1707), music: Robert Lowry (1867)
21:6; 22:13; 1:8	"Alpha and Omega," by Erasmus Mutanbira (2005, Sound of the New Breed)
21:9	"Beulah Land," words: Edgar P. Sites (1876), music: John R. Sweney (Isaiah

	62:4)
21:12-13, 21	"Twelve Gates to the City," African American spiritual
21:25	"Beyond the Sunset," by Virgil F. Brock and Blanche Kerr Brock (1936, 1964, The Rodehaver Co., a division of Word, Inc.)
21:33	"I Am Bound for the Promised Land" ("On Jordan's Stormy Banks, I Stand," words: Samuel Stennett (1787), music: Miss M. Durham (1835). Heb 11:16
22:1	"Shall We Gather at the River?" words and music: Robert Lowry (1864)
22:1	"Far Side Banks of Jordan," words: Tommy Smith (1976, Silverline Music)
22:1	"I'll Fly Away," Albert E. Brumley (1932, 1960, Albert E. Brumley and Sons, Psalm 90:10)
22:2	"In the Sweet By and By," words: Sanford F. Bennett (1868), music: Joseph P. Webster
22:4	"O That Will Be Glory," words and music: Charles H. Gabriel (1900)
22:4	"O I Want to See Him," words and music: Rufus Henry Cornelius (1916)
22:4	"When We See Christ" ("It Will Be Worth It All"), by Esther K. Rusthoi (1951)
22:4	"Face to Face with Christ, My Savior," words: Carrie E. Breck (1898), music: Grant C. Tullar (1 Cor 13:12)
22:4	"Saved by Grace," words: Fanny J. Crosby (1891) and George C. Stebbins (1894)
22:4	"We Shall See His Lovely Face," by Norman J. Clayton (1942, 1945, renewed 1971, 1973, by Norman Clayton Publishing Co. (a division of Word, Inc.)
22:13	"You Are Holy" ("Prince of Peace"), by Marc Imboden and Tammi Rhoton (1994, Imboden Music; Martha Jo Publishing)
22:14	"He the Pearly Gates Will Open," words: Frederick A. Blom (1917), translated from Swedish by Nathaniel Carlson (c. 1935), music attributed to Alfred Dulin (1930)

Appendix 3. Songs and Hymns Based on Revelation

22:17	"For Those Tears I Died" ("Come to the waters...."), by Marsha J. Stevens (1972, Bud John Songs, Inc.)
22:17	"All Who Are Thirsty," by Benton Brown and Glenn Robertson (1998, Vineyard Songs, UK/EIRE)
22:20	"Soon and Very Soon," by André Crouch (1971, Bud John Songs, Inc.)
22:20	"The King Is Coming!" by Charles Milhuff, Glory and Bill Gaither (1970, William J. Gaither Inc.)

CPSIA information can be obtained
at www.ICGtesting.com
Printed in the USA
BVHW011412040122
625206BV00004B/260